TONI BRANCATISANO

AN ITALIAN KITCHEN

A CELEBRATION OF SEASONAL AND TRADITIONAL ITALIAN CUISINE

THE MENTORIS PROJECT

To my mother, whose unwavering love and support continue to guide me from heaven.
You are the reason I fell in love with cooking and the art of presentation.

To my father: thank you for instilling in us a deep pride in our Italian heritage and all that it represents.
You taught me the value of hard work and showed me that true generosity knows no bounds.

To my sister, who patiently and thoughtfully critiqued every food photo and text.
Your dedication, talent, and boundless creativity inspire me every day. I am in awe of all that you achieve.

To my children, Annabella and Joseph, who make me proud every single day.
Watching you grow into such remarkable adults fills my heart with love. I am endlessly grateful for you both.

INTRODUCTION

BELLA ITALIA . . . ITALY, IL BEL PAESE . . . if you haven't yet visited this beautiful country, I'm sure it's on your bucket list. Whether it's to marvel at its ancient monuments, experience the charm of Italian beaches, or indulge in some shopping, one thing is certain—at the top of your list will be the food. Delicious, traditional, and unforgettable. If your priorities are in the right place, the monuments are simply a way to pass the time while you digest between breakfast, lunch, and dinner!

Whatever brings you to Italy, it will never disappoint. You'll find yourself needing to return again and again.

The food of Italy has a history as rich and wonderful as the country itself. It remains a culinary cornerstone across the world, evoking images of vibrant markets, fresh ingredients, and cherished family recipes. In fact, if you ask someone to name something quintessentially Italian, food is likely the first thing that comes to mind.

If you were lucky enough to grow up in an Italian family, your daily life inevitably revolved around food. It's often said, and it couldn't be truer: Food brings families together. Whether it's the noisy rush of breakfast before everyone heads off to work or school, an intimate dinner shared at home, or a boisterous family reunion where lively conversation dominates the table, food is always at the heart of it all.

When we think of an Italian family, the first image that comes to mind is surely that of a robust, happy, smiling, cheek-pinching *nonna*. An Italian nonna embodies everything there is to love about Italy and being Italian, often serving as the glue that holds the family together. Nonna is loving and opinionated and firmly believes she knows what's best. God forbid you disagree with her! She is a wife, a mother, and a grandmother, but she is also a chef and a baker, a family psychologist, and, of course, the family doctor, dispensing medical advice and cures for any ailment. Nonna will not hesitate to tell you she knows better than the local GP. You quickly learn that going to bed with wet hair, swimming too soon after eating, or getting "hit" by the *colpo d'aria* (a draft) might just be the end of you.

Nonna is the nurturer of the family, a role that still resonates today as many women in Italy work, leaving Nonna responsible for childcare. Her best way to nurture is through food, often feeding the children their after-school snack, a *merenda*. This could be as simple as a tomato freshly picked from the garden, rubbed over thick, crusty bread, and topped with a sprinkle of salt and a generous splash of extra-virgin olive oil—*pane e pomodoro* at its finest! Although this might be contested if children were treated to another once-popular merenda: bread with wine and sugar!

If you happen to visit Nonna just before lunch or dinner (a strategic plan often employed by children and grandchildren alike), she will first apologize, claiming she has no food in the house to offer you. Then, she will proceed to produce enough food for the entire street. She watches you eat, and when you're bursting at the seams, she will insist you have more. Every Italian knows that refusing food is an offense. We're taught from a young age that we mustn't offend, so even if you say no once, twice, or even three times, you will inevitably give in. This dance of refusal has been perfected over generations: You must say no a couple of times to allow Nonna to insist, but deep down, you both know you'll say yes to seconds or thirds. After all, Nonna's role in life is to give love, food, and affection.

Italian cuisine is a celebration of simplicity, respect for seasonal ingredients, and ancient traditions. Its beauty lies in its fresh, uncomplicated, and quick recipes that are relatively easy to put together. Whether you're hosting a large gathering or enjoying a cozy, intimate meal, Italian dishes are perfect for any occasion. Many of these recipes have humble origins in peasant kitchens, known as *la cucina povera*, where shepherds, peasants, and fishermen used their creativity to make the most of what was available. Eating is a sacred ritual in Italy, with each meal and hour taken seriously. The timing of meals is just as important as the food itself.

Within this book, you'll find a mix of well-known recipes and hidden gems, some famous only in specific regions of Italy. Despite their differences, they all share the ability to transport your taste buds to the heart of Italy—whether it's a tiny kitchen, a specific region, or a lively piazza where these recipes originated.

In Italy, cooking is an art form, but so is shopping. To recreate the magic of *la buona cucina Italiana*, it's essential to embrace the Italian way of shopping. Italians typically visit local markets or small, family-run stores almost daily, buying just what they need for the next two to three days. This habit isn't just about buying fresh ingredients—it's about celebrating seasonality and minimizing food waste.

You'll often see people at the bakery purchasing half or even a quarter of a loaf of bread, especially if they live alone. Traditional Italian bread is made without artificial preservatives, so it doesn't last long. This might sound like a drawback, but in reality, it's a marker of quality, a sign that the bread is free from additives. Compare that to industrially produced supermarket bread, which can sit in your pantry for days, seemingly untouched by time.

Moreover, Italians are masters of transforming leftovers into new, delicious dishes. Many of Italy's iconic recipes have humble beginnings, born from the creativity of turning yesterday's meal into tomorrow's feast.

In today's fast-paced world, maintaining the culinary traditions that are at the heart of Italian culture is becoming increasingly difficult. We live in a time where convenience often takes precedence, and as a result, many of the treasured family recipes that once defined *la cucina Italiana* are fading away. It's a bittersweet reality, especially for those who reflect on the loss of these recipes with the passing of beloved grandparents. How many of us now regret not taking the time to learn those recipes when Nonna was still in the kitchen, effortlessly preparing meals that held generations of tradition?

The real tragedy is not only the loss of these dishes, but also how they have evolved, sometimes straying far from their authentic origins, particularly among descendants of Italian emigrants. Once, it was a natural rite of passage for recipes to be passed down from generation to generation, often through the women of the family. There was no need to document them—they lived on in practice, taught by example in a rhythm of life that revolved around the family kitchen.

But today, many of us look back with regret, wishing we had paid more attention to our grandmothers. We realize too late how valuable that time spent cooking with Nonna would have been. If only someone had insisted that we join her, to help knead dough for pasta, bake bread, or prepare sauces from scratch. As children, we might have rolled our eyes at the suggestion, but as adults, we would give anything for those precious memories and the invaluable skills they would have imparted.

The essence of great Italian cooking lies not only in respecting the seasons, but also in keeping things simple and using the best-quality ingredients available. Most traditional Italian recipes are composed of just a few basic components, and the more we complicate them, the further we stray from the original culinary wisdom passed down through generations. It's this simplicity, combined with a deep respect for the integrity of each ingredient, that defines true Italian cuisine.

Getting recipes from Nonna wasn't always straightforward. Even those who could write didn't rely on exact measurements. Cooking wasn't learned from books but instead taught by observing, practicing, and hands-on experience. When asked for a recipe, Nonna might just shrug, offering guidance like a *pizzico* (pinch) or a handful, relying on intuition rather than precise amounts. One phrase that captures this beautifully is Q.B.—*quanto basta*, meaning "as needed." It's still used today for ingredients like salt or pepper, much like "to taste." The magic of Q.B. lies in its flexibility, reminding us that cooking is about personal instinct and adaptation while staying rooted in tradition.

The word "seasonality" is often mentioned today, but it truly defines the Italian kitchen. Italians have always respected the rhythm of the seasons, a tradition still evident in local *mercati* across Italy. Each season brings a cherished ingredient, and long-awaited recipes are joyfully revived. In fact, you don't need a calendar to track the time of year—just visit the market and let the produce guide you.

Take Lazio, for example, where late autumn and winter signal the arrival of artichokes. At the market, vendors skillfully clean artichokes for *carciofi alla romana* (Roman-style artichokes), trimming them with precision. As the discarded leaves pile up like purple-green petals, the refreshing scent of lemon fills the air, rubbed onto the freshly prepared artichoke heads. This sensory experience is part of the charm of Italian markets—sight, smell, taste, and even sound all play a role.

In summer, vibrant tomatoes and sweet peaches dominate, while autumn brings chestnuts, mushrooms, and persimmons. Winter ushers in the bright tang of citrus fruits and apples, and spring is greeted with the arrival of delicate wild asparagus and baby lamb, central to the Easter feast. Each season is a celebration, a reminder that Italian cuisine is deeply rooted in the natural cycle of life.

The seasons not only dictate when we eat certain foods, but also shape the recipes tied to the many festivals celebrated throughout Italy. Religious festivals play a fundamental role in Italian life, especially given that the Catholic Church represents the vast majority of Christians in the country. Even though many Italians today may not be active, practicing Catholics, the tradition of honoring saints and celebrating religious festivals—along with the food that accompanies these occasions—remains deeply ingrained in the culture.

These festivals and their accompanying dishes offer a powerful way to bring people together and reunite families, making food not just a part of the celebration, but the heart of it. Whether it's Christmas, Easter, or the feast of a local saint, each occasion is a reflection of Italy's rich history, where faith, tradition, and food unite to create lasting memories.

Italian family celebrations are filled with lively chatter, occasional disagreements, and most importantly, the delightful aromas, unforgettable flavors, and the love that brings everyone together. This book celebrates Italy, its people, their traditions, *le feste* (the celebrations), the wonderful recipes, and the legacy created by Italian grandmothers.

When I started writing this book, I was concerned that many Italian traditions were slowly fading away. However, during my research travels in Italy, I discovered the opposite. I found a strong desire to uphold family traditions and preserve ancestral recipes. Most of the people I interviewed came from families with a heritage of four or five generations running their family businesses. I hope that reading this book brings back nostalgic memories of a beloved family recipe, evokes beautiful moments spent with grandparents, reminds you of your favorite local Italian eatery, or transports you back to a past holiday in Italy. I also hope it inspires you to step into the kitchen and recreate the recipes within its pages, and most importantly, encourages you to book a flight and visit Italy soon.

A presto!

Toni

spring

CROCCHETTE DI PATATE

POTATO CROQUETTES

Potato croquettes are a beloved staple of Italian cuisine, particularly in Southern Italy. As with many traditional recipes, there are countless variations, allowing them to be as simple or indulgent as you like. They also offer a great way to make use of any leftovers in the fridge.

My Nonna Concetta would make these for our big family get-togethers, and the taste instantly brings back so many happy memories as soon as I pop one in my mouth. I'm sharing two versions here—one with a breadcrumb coating and one without. *Crocchette* are perfect not only as an *aperitivo*, but also as a versatile side dish for any main meal. They're delicious hot, yet equally enjoyable warm or cold, making them ideal for buffets and parties.

YIELD 1 1/2 TO 2 DOZEN, (DEPENDING ON THEIR SIZE)

8 russet potatoes, peeled and quartered

Salt

3 cups dry breadcrumbs (360 g)

1 cup freshly grated Pecorino Romano (100 g)

4 eggs

1 cup ham (150 g), finely chopped

1/2 cup fresh flat-leaf parsley (20 g), finely chopped

Freshly cracked black pepper

Flour

Olive oil, for frying

Place potatoes in a large saucepan of salted water. Bring to a boil and simmer 30 minutes, or until potatoes are very tender. Drain and let cool completely.

Pass potatoes through a potato ricer into a large bowl. Stir in 1 cup breadcrumbs, cheese, 2 eggs, ham, and parsley. Season to taste with salt and freshly cracked black pepper. Form the potato mixture into sausage-like croquettes.

In 3 separate wide, shallow bowls or large plates, place flour, remaining 2 eggs (lightly beaten), and remaining 2 cups breadcrumbs, forming an assembly line. Dredge each croquette in flour, dip in egg, and coat in breadcrumbs.

Heat olive oil in a deep fryer or large heavy-bottomed pan. Fry the croquettes, turning frequently until golden. Remove and drain on paper towels.

My Nonna Concetta made crocchette without the breadcrumb coating. She would form the potato mixture into 1 1/2-inch balls, gently flatten them, coat each one in flour, and fry as above.

VIGNAROLA

Nothing celebrates spring vegetables better than this wonderfully versatile Roman dish. It can complement a hearty meat dish or be savored on its own with a slice of toasted, crusty bread.

SERVES 4

5 artichokes, cleaned

Juice of 1 lemon

5 ounces pancetta (150 g), sliced

Extra-virgin olive oil

2 large red onions, chopped

1/2 cup white wine (120 ml)

2 to 3 cups vegetable broth (480 to 720 ml) (see recipe on page 210)

Salt

2 cups fresh peas (300 g), shelled

2 cups fava beans (300 g), shelled and peeled

1 head romaine, roughly chopped

Freshly grated Pecorino Romano cheese, to serve

Freshly cracked black pepper, to serve

Remove and discard the stalks and outer leaves from artichokes to reveal the tender inner parts. Cut artichokes in quarters, soak in water with lemon juice, and set aside.

Sauté pancetta in a heavy-bottomed pan until golden. Add a generous splash of olive oil and chopped onions. Cook until onions are translucent. Add wine and drained artichokes. Cover and simmer 10 minutes.

Uncover and add 2 cups broth and a pinch of salt. Add peas and fava beans and cook 15 minutes.

Add romaine. Season to taste with salt and pepper and add more stock, if needed. Cover and simmer over low heat 5 minutes. Turn off the heat and let rest about 1 hour before serving warm. This allows all the flavors to combine better.

Sprinkle freshly grated Pecorino Romano and pepper over each serving.

Given to Roman soldiers as part of their daily rations, Pecorino Romano is one of Italy's oldest cheeses. Not to be confused with Romano cheese, which is made from cow's milk, Pecorino Romano is a hard, salty cheese made from sheep's milk and holds a Protected Designation of Origin status in the European Union. Only cheese produced in certain areas and following specific methods can be labeled Pecorino Romano. Pecorino Romano was traditionally buried in salt for its entire 10- to 12-month aging period, which is why it has a strong salty flavor.

SPAGHETTI AGLIO, OLIO E PEPERONCINO

SPAGHETTI WITH GARLIC, OLIVE OIL, AND CHILI PEPPER

This recipe is a lifesaver when it feels like there's nothing to cook in the house. Spaghetti with garlic, extra-virgin olive oil, and chili pepper is a first course that is very easy and quick to prepare—in fact, it only takes the time to boil the water and cook the spaghetti. Adding salt to the pasta water is very important for the final flavor of this dish, so don't forget this important step.

Make sure you use a quality pasta, fragrant garlic, extra-virgin olive oil, and fresh chili peppers. By following just a few basic steps, you'll have one of the most famous and appreciated pasta dishes in Italian cuisine. Deciding whether to keep or remove the chili seeds comes down to your personal preference for how spicy you'd like your pasta.

SERVES 4

Salt

1 pound spaghetti (455 g)

1 bunch fresh flat-leaf parsley, leaves and stalks separated

Extra-virgin olive oil

2 cloves garlic, peeled and crushed

2 to 3 fresh chili peppers, sliced

Bring a large pot of salted water to a boil. Add spaghetti and cook for half the time stated in the package directions.

While the pasta cooks, finely chop the parsley leaves. Heat 1/2 cup olive oil in a large pan. Add garlic and about 5 parsley stalks. Stir frequently until the garlic turns a beautiful amber color. Be careful not to let the garlic burn as it will ruin the flavor of the dish. Remove the garlic and parsley.

Reduce the temperature and add sliced chilies.

Drain the very al dente pasta, reserving the water. Add the pasta to the pan and stir in 1 ladle of pasta water and chopped parsley leaves. Add more water as needed, stirring continually until the spaghetti is cooked. The starch released from the pasta combined with water and olive oil will create a lovely sauce.

GARGANELLI AL RAGÙ DI AGNELLO

GARGANELLI PASTA WITH LAMB RAGÙ

Traditional to the Emilia-Romagna region, *garganelli* is a tubular egg pasta that can be made at home. However, this ragù works really well with pappardelle too. Easy to make and rich in flavor, this makes a perfect *primo* for an Easter lunch.

SERVES 4

1/4 cup extra-virgin olive oil

1/4 cup (1/2 stick) unsalted butter (60 g)

1 carrot, finely chopped

1 rib celery, finely chopped

1 small onion, finely chopped

3/4 pound ground lamb (340 g)

1/4 pound ground veal (115 g)

1 cup white wine (240 ml)

1 cup broth of choice (240 ml) (see recipes on pages 210–211)

Salt and pepper

2 sprigs fresh rosemary

2 sprigs fresh thyme

1 pound garganelli (455 g)

1/4 cup freshly grated Parmigiano Reggiano (25 g), plus more to serve

Heat olive oil and 1 tablespoon butter in a saucepan. Add carrot, celery, and onion and sauté until onion is translucent.

Add lamb and veal and cook over high heat, breaking up the meat and stirring continually.

Add white wine and let reduce a little. Add broth, salt and pepper to taste, and fresh herbs. Cook, covered, over medium-low heat for about 1 hour. Stir occasionally and add more broth should the ragù become too dry.

Meanwhile, bring a large pot of salted water to a boil and cook garganelli about 10 minutes. Drain, reserving the pasta water, and return pasta to the same saucepan. Add the ragù, remaining 3 tablespoons butter, and 1/4 cup Parmigiano Reggiano, and stir over low heat until butter has melted and incorporated into the sauce. If the ragù is too dry, add a little pasta water.

Serve immediately, sprinkled with Parmigiano Reggiano.

A ragù is a rich, slow-cooked sauce made with meat, vegetables, and sometimes tomatoes, though the ingredients can vary by region. Typically, ground beef, pork, and/or veal is slowly cooked with onions, carrots, celery, and sometimes garlic to create a rich, hearty sauce.

GNUDI

SPINACH AND RICOTTA DUMPLINGS

Gnudi are a favored Tuscan comfort food. Typical of *cucina povera*—peasant cooking—the ingredients are simple and native to the region. In the Tuscan dialect, *gnudo* means "naked," an appropriate name because gnudi are the filling of ravioli without the pasta covering; one could say that gnudi are ravioli stripped naked.

The recipe below offers the traditional way to enjoy gnudi. However, you can pair them with any sauce, much like gnocchi. If you have any leftovers, place them in a baking dish and cover with a simple tomato sauce, mozzarella, and Parmigiano Reggiano. Bake at 375°F (190°C) until the cheese is golden and bubbly. You'll never feel like you're eating leftovers again.

SERVES 4

2 pounds fresh spinach (900 g), rinsed

1 3/4 cup sheep's or cow's milk ricotta (425 g), well drained

2 eggs

1 cup freshly grated Parmigiano Reggiano (100 g), plus more to serve

1/3 cup all-purpose flour (40 g), plus more for dredging

1/2 teaspoon nutmeg, freshly grated, plus more to serve

1/2 teaspoon freshly cracked black pepper

Salt

1/2 cup (1 stick) unsalted butter (110 g)

8 to 10 fresh sage leaves

Bring water to a boil in a saucepan. Add spinach and simmer 5 minutes. Drain and squeeze well to remove excess water. Chop finely with a knife or food processor and let cool.

Mix ricotta, eggs, 1 cup Parmigiano Reggiano, 1/3 cup flour, 1/2 teaspoon nutmeg, and pepper in a large bowl. Stir in chopped spinach and salt to taste.

Prepare a bowl of flour for dredging. Rub some flour on your hands and shape the spinach mixture into 1 1/2-inch balls. They don't need to be perfectly round. If too sticky to handle, shape using two spoons. Roll the formed balls in flour and let stand 30 minutes.

Bring a large pot of salted water to a boil. Heat a second pan over medium-high heat and add butter and sage leaves. When butter melts, turn off heat.

Place gnudi, a few at a time, in boiling water. As soon as they rise to the surface, remove with a slotted spoon and transfer to the pan with melted butter.

When the pan is full, return to medium-high heat. Gently toss gnudi until butter bubbles and sage leaves appear slightly fried.

Serve gnudi with the melted butter and sprinkle with grated Parmigiano Reggiano and nutmeg.

Gnudi can be refrigerated, formed, uncooked, and covered up to 12 hours. They can also be frozen for about 1 month and boiled straight from the freezer.

RAVIOLI RICOTTA E SPINACI

SPINACH AND RICOTTA RAVIOLI

Spring is the perfect time to indulge in ricotta cheese, when it is at its peak. Ravioli filled with spinach and ricotta is a classic dish that typically needs little more than a drizzle of olive oil and a sprinkle of Parmigiano Reggiano. Celebrate the season by elevating this dish with the addition of spring peas, fresh basil, and crispy pancetta.

SERVES 4

Salt

1 pound fresh spinach (455 g), rinsed

1 3/4 cups sheep's or cow's milk ricotta (425 g), well drained

1 egg

1 tablespoon freshly grated Parmigiano Reggiano, plus more to serve

Freshly cracked black pepper

Egg pasta (see recipe on page 219)

1/2 cup peas (70 g)

2 ounces pancetta (50 g), diced

Olive oil

1 bunch fresh flat-leaf parsley, roughly chopped

5 to 6 fresh basil leaves, roughly chopped

FOR THE FILLING: Bring a pot of salted water to a boil. Blanch spinach 2 minutes. Drain and squeeze well to remove excess water. Chop in a food processor or blender. Mix spinach, ricotta, egg, 1 tablespoon Parmigiano Reggiano, salt, and pepper in a bowl. Spoon into a piping bag and refrigerate until needed.

ASSEMBLE THE RAVIOLI (see instructions on page 222).

FOR THE FINAL DISH: Bring a saucepan of water to a boil and cook peas. Drain and place under cold running water to prevent peas from overcooking. Set aside.

Bring a large pot of salted water to a boil. Add ravioli. Avoid stirring to prevent breakage. Maintain a gentle boil 5 to 6 minutes. Test readiness by sampling a piece retrieved with a slotted spoon.

While the ravioli cooks, sauté pancetta in a large pan until golden.

Drain ravioli and transfer to the pan with pancetta. Add a splash of olive oil and reserved peas. Leave on stovetop just long enough to heat peas. Remove from heat and stir in chopped parsley and basil. Sprinkle with Parmigiano Reggiano and a little freshly cracked black pepper and serve immediately.

RAVIOLI DI ASPARAGI E FORMAGGIO DI CAPRA CON BURRO, SALVIA E NOCCIOLE

ASPARAGUS AND GOAT CHEESE RAVIOLI WITH BURNT BUTTER, SAGE, AND HAZELNUTS

A wonderful way to celebrate seasonal asparagus, especially the wild variety that graces Italian markets at this time of year. The marriage of earthy asparagus, creamy goat cheese, nutty browned butter, fragrant sage, and crunchy hazelnuts creates a truly unforgettable dish—one that's perfect for a special occasion or simply savoring the best of spring.

SERVES 4 TO 6

1 pound asparagus (455 g)

Salt

Freshly cracked black pepper

8 ounces soft goat cheese (225 g), plus more to serve

8 ounces sheep's or cow's milk ricotta (200 g), well drained

1/4 cup Pecorino Romano (25 g), finely grated

Egg pasta (see recipe on page 219)

1 cup (2 sticks) salted butter (225 g)

20 fresh sage leaves

1 cup whole hazelnuts (135 g), roasted and chopped

Zest of 1 lemon to serve (optional)

Goat cheese to serve (optional)

Wash asparagus and cut tips to 2-inch lengths and set aside. Snap the tough ends from asparagus and discard.

FOR THE FILLING: Chop remaining asparagus stalks into small pieces. Place in a shallow pan with salt and pepper and cover with 2 cups water. Bring to a boil. Reduce heat and simmer until asparagus is soft and water has evaporated. Put aside to cool and then purée in a food processor or blender until smooth.

Mix goat cheese, ricotta, and Pecorino Romano in a bowl. Add freshly cracked black pepper. Stir in puréed asparagus. Taste. If you think it needs more salt, try adding some Pecorino Romano instead. Spoon into a piping bag and refrigerate until needed.

ASSEMBLE THE RAVIOLI (see instructions on page 222).

FOR THE FINAL DISH: Bring a large pot of salted water to a boil and fill a large bowl with ice water. Blanch reserved asparagus tips in boiling water for a short amount of time. Transfer to the ice water bath and set aside.

Place a medium nonstick pan over medium-low heat and add butter and sage. When butter has melted, raise the heat to medium-high and bring it to a robust simmer. Add hazelnuts and cook until butter is golden brown and sage is crisp. Add blanched and drained asparagus tips and stir to coat in butter.

Meanwhile, bring a large pot of salted water to a boil. Add ravioli. Avoid stirring to prevent breakage. Maintain a gentle boil 8 to 10 minutes, adjusting for pasta thickness. Test readiness by sampling a piece retrieved with a slotted spoon.

Once the ravioli are cooked, use a slotted spoon to transfer to the pan with the butter sauce. Toss quickly over medium heat to ensure ravioli are thoroughly coated in the sage butter. Garnish with lemon zest and a few dabs of goat cheese, if desired, and serve.

CONCHIGLIONI CON RICOTTA E LIMONE

SHELL PASTA WITH RICOTTA AND LEMON

There's no better way to celebrate springtime ricotta than by simply tossing it with freshly cooked pasta. That said, this recipe is equally perfect for summer—light, fresh, and requiring little cooking at all. In the time it takes to boil the pasta, you can whip up a truly delicious and satisfying meal. I prefer using large pasta shells, which allow the ricotta to nestle perfectly in the crevices, but any pasta shape will do. Be careful with the mint; it should enhance the delicate flavors of the ricotta and lemon zest, not overpower them.

SERVES 4

Salt

1 pound short pasta, such as shells, penne, rigatoni, or fusilli (455 g)

1 cup sheep's or cow's milk ricotta (250 g), well drained

Zest of 2 lemons

1 bunch fresh mint

Freshly cracked black pepper

Bring a large pot of salted water to a boil. Add pasta and cook 2 minutes less than package directions until al dente.

Push ricotta through a sieve into a bowl. Add zest of 1 lemon and 1 tablespoon finely chopped mint. Season to taste with salt and pepper.

Drain pasta, reserving the water, and return the pasta to the saucepan. Add the ricotta mixture and stir until the pasta is thoroughly coated. Stir in just enough reserved pasta water to create a smooth, creamy sauce. Don't add too much as the sauce should be rich and creamy, not watery.

Garnish with remaining zest of 1 lemon, some small mint leaves, and freshly cracked black pepper, and serve immediately.

When making pasta, it's always a good idea to save some of the pasta water. The starchy water helps emulsify the sauce, creating a smoother, more cohesive mixture and ensuring the sauce clings perfectly to the pasta. In this recipe, you might need less than 1/2 cup—or even none at all—depending on the consistency of the ricotta.

FETTUCCINE AL RAGÙ

FETTUCCINE WITH BOLOGNESE SAUCE

SERVES 4

7 ounces diced guanciale or pancetta (200 g)

4 ribs celery, finely chopped

2 medium onions, finely chopped

2 large carrots, finely chopped

1/3 cup olive oil

1 pound ground beef (455 g)

1 pound ground Italian pork sausage (455 g)

1 cup red wine (240 ml)

4 (14-ounce) cans crushed tomatoes (400 g)

1 cup broth (240 ml) (see recipe on page 211)

2 tablespoons tomato paste

5 to 6 fresh basil leaves

2 bay leaves

1 tablespoon fresh rosemary

Salt

Freshly cracked black pepper

1 pound fettuccine (455 g)

Freshly grated Parmigiano Reggiano, to serve

Place guanciale, celery, onions, and carrots in a large ovenproof saucepan with the olive oil. Sauté over medium-low heat, stirring occasionally for about 10 minutes, or until onions are translucent and guanciale is golden.

Add ground beef and sausage. Stir, breaking up meat with a wooden spoon until mostly browned. Stir in red wine and let reduce. Add canned tomatoes, broth, tomato paste, basil, bay leaves, and rosemary. Stir and season well with salt and pepper.

Bring to a boil before reducing to a gentle simmer for 1 hour. Stir occasionally to ensure the sauce doesn't burn and stick to the base of the saucepan.

Preheat oven to 300°F (150°C).

Transfer ragù to preheated oven. Cover and cook 2 hours until sauce is thick. Remove bay leaves.

Bring a large pot of salted water to a boil. Add pasta and cook according to the package directions or until al dente.

Place 2 cups ragù in a large pan over medium-low heat. Using a slotted spoon, add the fettuccine to the pan. Toss well and stir to ensure all the pasta is coated with the sauce.

Sprinkle with freshly grated Parmigiano Reggiano and serve.

This recipe makes around 3 quarts (3 L) of sauce, so you will have plenty left over which you can freeze.

SALTIMBOCCA ALLA ROMANA

In Italian, *saltimbocca* means "jump in the mouth" and you'll understand why when you taste it. Saltimbocca is made from veal, slices of prosciutto, and sage. It is a classic Roman recipe and one you'll find in most restaurants in the Eternal City. Few ingredients are required to create a flavorful dish, and we have the prosciutto crudo to thank for that! In Italy, when you ask for prosciutto, they will ask you what type of prosciutto you want. They are asking you to differentiate between prosciutto *crudo* and prosciutto *cotto*. Cotto (cooked) is basically what we call ham. Crudo (cured), commonly known as Parma ham, is often served thinly sliced as an appetizer (think prosciutto and melon) or added to pasta dishes.

SERVES 3

6 veal escalopes, lean and thinly sliced

1 cup flour (120 g)

Salt and pepper

6 to 12 slices prosciutto crudo

6 to 8 fresh sage leaves

1/2 cup (1 stick) unsalted butter (110 g)

Extra-virgin olive oil

3/4 cup white wine (180 ml)

Place veal cutlets between 2 pieces of parchment paper and pound with a meat tenderizer until they are about 1/4-inch thick. This may not be necessary if veal is already thinly sliced.

Place flour in a wide, shallow bowl or large plate, and stir in 1 teaspoon salt and 1 teaspoon pepper. Coat veal in seasoned flour, shaking off excess.

Put 1 to 2 slices of prosciutto on each cutlet. Lay 1 sage leaf on top, and secure by weaving a toothpick in and out of each escalope.

Heat a large pan over medium heat and add butter and a generous splash of olive oil. You can also add a couple of sage leaves if you like.

Place half the veal in the pan, prosciutto-side down, and cook about 3 minutes or until prosciutto looks golden. Turn and cook about 2 minutes longer. Remove from the pan and set aside. Repeat with the remaining meat.

Return the cooked veal to the pan. Add wine and swirl around pan. Let reduce to create a lovely sauce to serve with the saltimbocca.

AGNELLO ARROSTO CON PANCETTA E PATATE AL FORNO

ROAST LAMB WITH PANCETTA AND POTATOES

Lamb is a beloved dish on tables across Italy, especially in the spring. It's particularly celebrated during the festive Easter season. This recipe is not only packed with flavor, but also makes an impressive presentation, perfect for entertaining and wowing family and friends. In Italy, *abbacchio*—young lamb—is much smaller than the lambs found in America, Australia, or New Zealand. The first time I bought a leg of lamb, I discovered there was barely enough meat for two people. I quickly learned that in Italy, legs and shoulders are often cooked together to provide plenty for a family meal. Plan for about 1 pound of uncooked meat per person, and roast for approximately 20 minutes per pound.

SERVES 6

Salt

2 pounds potatoes (900 g), unpeeled

2 tablespoons fresh rosemary leaves

2 tablespoons fresh thyme leaves

3 cloves garlic and 2 bulbs garlic

1 1/2 teaspoons rock salt

1/4 cup olive oil (60 ml)

1 (4-pound) bone-in leg of lamb or lamb shoulder (1.8 kg)

8 to 10 slices pancetta or bacon

Preheat oven to 350°F (180°C).

Bring a large pot of salted water to a boil. Wash potatoes and cut them into 1 1/2-inch pieces. Place in boiling water and cook about 10 minutes until they are a little soft.

In a food processor, chop rosemary, thyme, 3 garlic cloves and rock salt. Pour in the olive oil. Process roughly to create a rub for the lamb.

With a sharp knife, make cuts in the meat and massage the herb rub all over. Lay pancetta or bacon slices on top of the lamb. Secure with kitchen string.

Place lamb in a roasting pan and surround with potatoes. Cut garlic bulbs in half horizontally and add to pan, sliced side down.

Bake at 350°F (180°C) for about 1 hour and 20 minutes, or until a thermometer inserted into thickest part of lamb registers 130°F (55°C). Remove lamb from the oven, and while it rests for 15 minutes, continue to cook the potatoes if you prefer them more golden.

COTOLETTA ALLA MILANESE

One of Milan's signature dishes, *cotoletta alla milanese* dates back to the twelfth century. This breaded veal cutlet is also known as *costoletta alla milanese*. Some distinguish between the two by saying cotoletta is boneless, while costoletta includes the bone. Since "ribs" in Italian is *costole*, it makes sense to call it costoletta if it has a lovely bone attached. To stay true to tradition, the meat must come from the loin, with only the first six cutlets being suitable. These cutlets should also have the ideal amount of fat—not too lean and not too fatty.

SERVES 4

2 eggs

3 cups fresh breadcrumbs (180 g)

4 bone-in veal cutlets, 1-inch thick

3/4 cup (1 1/2 sticks) unsalted butter (170 g), preferably clarified

Salt, to serve

1 bunch fresh flat-leaf parsley, to serve

1 lemon, cut in wedges, to serve

Snip the membrane that surrounds each piece of veal in 3 or 4 places to prevent the meat from curling while it cooks.

Using a fork or whisk, beat eggs in a wide, shallow bowl or large plate. Place breadcrumbs in a separate wide, shallow bowl or large plate. Dip each cutlet in eggs, ensuring they are completely coated. Dredge in breadcrumbs, pressing down and turning over a couple of times to ensure the entire cutlet is coated.

Melt butter in a large, deep pan over medium-high heat. Sauté each cutlet about 15 minutes, turning only once, halfway through, until each side is golden, or to an internal temperature of 145°F (63°C). You may have to cook them in batches so they aren't crowded in the pan.

To serve, sprinkle with salt and, if desired, garnish with a little parsley and a couple of lemon wedges.

Avoid food waste by pulsing day-old rustic bread in a food processor to make your own breadcrumbs. They're always so much better than the finely ground, store-bought variety.

TORTA PASQUALINA

SAVORY EASTER TART

Torta pasqualina is more akin to a savory pie or quiche than a traditional *torta*. Originating in Genoa, it's a beloved dish prepared during Easter to celebrate the arrival of spring.

SERVES 8

3 1/2 cups all-purpose flour (420 g), sifted, plus more for rolling out dough

6 tablespoons (3/4 stick) unsalted butter (85 g), melted

11 eggs

Salt

Olive oil

4 artichoke hearts, sliced

2 sprigs fresh rosemary

1 clove garlic, peeled and chopped

Pepper

2 pounds fresh spinach (900 g)

1/4 cup freshly grated Parmigiano Reggiano (25 g)

2 sprigs fresh marjoram

1 cup sheep's or cow's milk ricotta (400 g), well drained

2/3 cup heavy cream (160 ml)

Place flour, butter, 2 eggs, a pinch of salt, and 1/4 cup warm water in a large bowl. Mix to form a ball of dough. Knead until smooth and elastic. Divide dough into 4 balls and return to the bowl. Cover with a slightly moistened cloth and let rest in a cool spot about 1 hour.

Preheat oven to 350°F (180°C).

Heat 2 tablespoons olive oil in a medium pan over medium heat. Add artichokes, rosemary, garlic, and salt and pepper to taste, and sauté 10 minutes. Set aside.

Cook spinach in a large saucepan with a little water, salt, and pepper until wilted. Cool, drain, and squeeze out excess water. Chop and transfer to a large bowl. Add Parmigiano Reggiano, marjoram leaves, ricotta, sautéed artichokes, salt, and pepper and mix well.

Lightly beat 3 eggs with an electric mixer and stir into the spinach mixture.

On a lightly floured surface, roll out 1 ball of dough to form a very thin sheet. Place on the bottom and sides of an oiled 9 1/2-inch (24-cm) cake pan. Brush the sheet with olive oil. Roll out a second ball of dough until very thin and place it on top of the first sheet, pressing it down to adhere well.

Spread spinach and ricotta mixture in the pan, leveling it with the back of a spoon. Using the spoon, create 6 indentations in the mixture and fill each with 1 egg, being careful not to break the yolks.

Repeat the process of rolling out the remaining balls of dough to create 2 more sheets of pastry. Cover the mixture with 1 pastry sheet, brush with olive oil, and cover with remaining sheet. Press the edges of the bottom and top layers of pastry together. If the pastry has become dry, use a little water to create a good seal. Finally, brush the top with olive oil.

Pierce the top with a fork and bake at 350°F (180°C) for 40 to 45 minutes, or until the top is golden. Can be served hot or cold.

CICORIA RIPASSATA

SAUTÉED ROMAN-STYLE CHICORY

If there's one thing Italians excel at, it's creating extraordinary vegetable side dishes. *Cicoria ripassata* is a staple on most Roman restaurant menus and is as versatile as it is delicious. It can be served as a side dish, added to pizza, used as a panini filling, tossed with pasta, or even folded into a flavorful frittata.

Chicory comes in several varieties, such as radicchio, Belgian endive, and frisée. For this recipe, I use puntarelle, which is grown in the Lazio region near my home in Rome. I love knowing that the produce I buy hasn't traveled far to reach my local market. Wild chicory leaves have a pleasantly bitter taste—though some are more bitter than others. The bitterness can be reduced by cooking the chicory twice: first by boiling, then by frying. In fact, *ripassata* means "cooked again."

SERVES 2 AS A SIDE DISH

Salt

1 1/2 pounds chicory (680 g)

1/4 cup olive oil (60 ml)

1 clove garlic, peeled

1 small fresh chili pepper, chopped

3 anchovy filets

Bring a large pot of salted water to a boil.

Remove and discard stalks from chicory and wash the leaves in cold water. Cook chicory in boiling water about 10 minutes. Drain, cool, and squeeze well to remove excess water.

Heat olive oil in a large pan over medium heat. Add whole garlic clove, chopped chili, and anchovies. Stir until anchovies dissolve into the olive oil.

When garlic is golden, add chicory leaves and toss in the pan about 5 minutes over high heat, ensuring chicory is thoroughly coated in the sauce. Remove garlic. Taste and season to taste with salt if needed. Serve hot or warm.

CASATIELLO NAPOLETANO

Casatiello napoletano is a savory bread traditionally served during Easter celebrations. It features a rich mix of cheeses—such as Grana Padano, Parmigiano Reggiano, Pecorino, and provolone—and salumi (cured meats) like salami, coppa, prosciutto, and ham. A classic touch is the placement of whole chicken eggs (shells intact) on top of the bread, secured with crisscrossed strips of dough, similar to *scarcella pugliese* (see page 43). However, I prefer to serve boiled quail eggs on the side for a more impressive presentation for guests.

Delicious whether served hot, warm, or cold, casatiello napoletano is a versatile option for breakfast, lunch, dinner, or even a snack. It's so irresistible that it's hard not to overindulge in one sitting! You may find, as I do, that this bread deserves to be enjoyed year-round—not just at Easter.

SERVES 10 TO 12

8 quail eggs, hard-boiled, peeled, and halved (plus more to serve, optional)

1/2 cup pork lard (100 g), plus more for greasing pan

8 cups all-purpose flour (960 g), plus more for rolling out dough

Salt

1 tablespoon freshly cracked black pepper

1/4 ounce fresh brewer's yeast (7 g)

8 ounces Pecorino Romano (225 g), diced

4 ounces fontina cheese (115 g), diced

4 ounces aged provolone (115 g), diced

1 3/4 cups salumi (any combination of salami, coppa, prosciutto, and ham), diced (400 g)

Place quail eggs in a small saucepan and cover with cold water. Bring to a gentle boil and cook 2 to 3 minutes. Transfer to a bowl of ice water and set aside.

Preheat oven to 350°F (180°C). Generously grease bottom and sides of a 12-inch (30-cm) tube pan with lard.

Sift flour on a work surface or into a large bowl of an electric mixer with a dough hook attached. Add a pinch of salt and pepper.

Dissolve yeast in 1/2 cup (120 ml) lukewarm water and stir into the flour, adding a little at a time. Slowly incorporate up to 2 cups water until a soft dough begins to form. Add 1/4 cup lard and thoroughly work it into the dough. Continue kneading dough approximately 10 minutes until it becomes slightly sticky and very elastic. Place in a clean bowl greased with lard. Cover with a kitchen towel and let rise 2 hours, or until doubled in volume.

Mix cheeses and salumi in a bowl. Divide in two and knead one portion into the risen dough.

On a lightly floured surface, roll out the dough into a rectangle. Brush lightly with lard and cover with remaining cheese and salumi mixture. Arrange peeled and halved quail eggs on top. Fold dough and shape into a long log. Bring the ends together to form a ring that will fit into the pan.

Gently place the dough in the prepared pan. Brush the top generously with more lard. Cover with a kitchen towel and let rise 2 hours.

Bake at 350°F (180°C) for 1 hour, or until top is golden. Serve with hard-boiled peeled quail eggs, if desired.

You can replace quail eggs with chicken eggs, adjusting the quantities.

PASTIERA NAPOLETANA

NEAPOLITAN EASTER TART

SERVES 8

FOR THE PASTRY

2 1/2 sticks unsalted butter (300 g)

4 cups all-purpose flour (480 g), plus more for rolling out dough

1 1/2 cups confectioners' sugar (180 g)

Zest of 1 orange

2 eggs, lightly beaten

FOR THE FILLING

1 1/2 cups sheep's or cow's milk ricotta (350 g), well drained

1 cup sugar (200 g)

1/2 cup custard

3 eggs

1 1/2 cups grano cotto (300 g)

2 cups candied orange peel (310 g)

2 teaspoons orange blossom water

2 teaspoons limoncello (optional)

Make custard for the filling well in advance so it has time to cool. (Please refer to the custard recipe for the fig tart on page 88.)

To make the pastry, cut cold butter into cubes. Combine flour and confectioners' sugar in a food processor. Add butter and pulse until the mixture resembles coarse breadcrumbs. Add orange zest and eggs. Mix until a dough begins to form.

On a lightly floured surface, gently knead dough into a ball. Flatten slightly, cover with plastic wrap, and refrigerate at least 40 minutes.

When ready, roll out the dough on a lightly floured surface. Cover the bottom and sides of a 2-inch-deep, 9 1/2-inch (24-cm) tart pan (or multiple small pans to make individual tarts as seen on the opposite page) with a removable bottom (or a springform pan). Place pan in refrigerator.

Roll out remaining dough between 2 pieces of parchment paper and refrigerate.

Preheat oven to 350°F (180°C).

To make the filling, beat ricotta and sugar with an electric mixer on medium speed until combined. With the mixer running, add 1/2 cup cold custard and eggs, one at a time, mixing well after each addition.

Stir in grano cotto, candied orange peel, orange blossom water, and, if desired, 2 teaspoons limoncello.

Pour into prepared crust. Cut the remaining pastry into narrow strips and create a lattice pattern on top.

Bake at 350°F (180°C) for 45 minutes to 1 hour. Remove when filling is slightly firm to the touch and pastry and filling are golden brown.

Let sit on a wire rack 30 minutes before removing from pan. Bring to room temperature and refrigerate. Dust with confectioners' sugar before serving.

ZUPPA INGLESE

ITALIAN TRIFLE

This recipe's origins date back to the Renaissance, but it wasn't until the nineteenth century that *zuppa inglese*, as we know it today, emerged in the cities of Ferrara and Bologna. As the name suggests, this "English soup"—layered with cake, custard, and liqueur—was likely inspired by Italian travelers to Britain who returned home with a taste for trifle.

Like many Italian dishes, zuppa inglese has numerous variations. It can be made with sponge cake, an Emilian sweet called *bensone*, or, more traditionally, *savoiardi* (ladyfingers) dipped in alchermes or rosolio liqueur. Alchermes, with its sweet, spicy, and slightly floral flavor, gives the dessert a striking hot pink hue.

In the recipe below, I've diluted the liqueur with sugar syrup to lower the alcohol content for children. However, if you're serving adults only, I recommend using the alchermes undiluted for a fuller flavor.

SERVES 6 TO 8

9 egg yolks

2 cups sugar (400 g)

2/3 cup flour (80 g)

1 quart whole milk (1 L)

2 strips peel of 1 lemon

1 vanilla bean, split lengthwise

1/3 cup unsweetened cocoa powder (40 g), sifted

1 cup alchermes liqueur (240 ml)

1 (7-ounce) packet savoiardi (ladyfingers) (200 g)

Grated dark chocolate, to serve

Whipped cream, to serve (optional)

In a medium bowl, whisk yolks and 1 1/2 cups sugar. Add flour and whisk until completely combined.

Place milk, lemon peel, and vanilla bean in a large saucepan over medium heat and bring to a boil. Remove from heat and discard lemon peel and vanilla bean.

Whisk 1 ladle hot milk into egg yolk mixture. Repeat until half the milk is incorporated. Then transfer to the saucepan with the remaining hot milk. Bring to a boil. When the custard has thickened, remove from heat and divide between 2 bowls. Stir cocoa powder into one and leave the other plain. Cover the bowls with plastic wrap, letting the plastic touch the surface of the custard to prevent a film from developing. Bring to room temperature. Refrigerate until needed.

Bring 3/4 cup water and remaining 1/2 cup sugar to a boil in a small saucepan. Stir until it forms a syrup. Remove from heat and add alchermes. Let cool.

In a large bowl or individual serving dishes, assemble the dessert in layers. Start with a layer of savoiardi quickly dipped into the alchermes syrup—about 2 seconds per side so they don't dissolve. Cover with chocolate custard. Place a layer of alchermes-soaked savoiardi perpendicular to the previous layer. Top with plain custard. Repeat layers, finishing with plain custard topped with alchermes-soaked savoiardi.

Cover with plastic wrap and refrigerate 2 hours, or until well chilled.

To serve, sprinkle some grated dark chocolate on top. For an extra touch, add a dollop of whipped cream, if desired.

CANNOLI

Italy boasts many culinary icons, but few are as beloved and iconic as Sicilian cannoli. In Italy, cannoli are traditionally made with ricotta from sheep's milk, which must be extremely fresh. This specific type of ricotta can sometimes be challenging to find outside of Italy, so cow's milk ricotta can absolutely be used as a substitute.

YIELD 5 DOZEN

3 1/4 cups all-purpose flour (390 g), plus more for rolling out dough

2 cups sugar (400 g)

2 tablespoons unsweetened cocoa powder

Salt

1/3 cup lard (70 g)

3 eggs (2 whole eggs and 1 white)

1/4 cup dry Marsala (60 ml)

1/4 cup white vinegar (60 ml)

Oil or lard for frying

4 1/2 pounds sheep's or cow's milk ricotta (2 kg), well drained

Ground cinnamon or vanilla extract

1 cup mini dark chocolate chips (150 g), plus more to decorate

Candied cherries, candied orange peel, or chopped pistachios, and confectioners' sugar, to decorate

Stir flour, 1/4 cup sugar, cocoa, and a pinch of salt in a large bowl. Add lard and mix well. Mix in 2 whole eggs until a dough forms. Add Marsala and vinegar and knead until well blended. Form into a ball, cover with plastic wrap, and refrigerate 1 hour, or until well chilled.

On a lightly floured surface, roll out the dough as thinly as you can. Or better yet, use a pasta machine, if you have one. Lightly dust the work surface and dough frequently with flour to keep the dough from sticking.

Cut out multiple circles from the dough with a 4-inch (10-cm) round cookie cutter. Gently pull each piece into an oval with your hands.

Wrap each oval of dough around a cannoli tube. Seal the overlapping dough with the egg white, pressing well to ensure it stays intact.

Fry, two at a time, in plenty of hot oil at 375°F (190°C) until the dough bubbles and blisters and turns golden brown. Carefully remove with tongs and drain on paper towels. When cool enough to handle, gently twist and remove the metal forms to release the shells.

Mix ricotta and remaining 1 3/4 cups sugar. Add a pinch of cinnamon or 1/2 teaspoon vanilla extract and refrigerate 1 hour, or until well chilled.

Push the ricotta through a wire sieve and divide between two bowls. Stir chocolate chips into one and leave the other plain.

A few minutes before serving, place the ricotta in piping bags and fill the cannoli shells.

Decorate each end as desired and sprinkle the shells with confectioners' sugar.

The number of shells produced by this recipe will vary based on the thickness of the rolled dough and the size of your cannoli molds.

SCARCELLA PUGLIESE

In Southern Italy, Easter wouldn't be complete without the traditional sweet pastries known as *scarcella* in Puglia, *cuzzupe* in Calabria, and *cuddura cu l'ova* in Sicily. Though they go by many names, these classic holiday treats are remarkably similar in both recipe and presentation.

Years ago, when chocolate eggs were a rare luxury few could afford, it was often the nonnas who prepared these cookies for their grandchildren as a delightful surprise to be enjoyed on Easter morning. According to tradition, these pastries are decorated with hard-boiled eggs, symbolizing the birth of new life and the pastry strips laid over the eggs are a clear reference to the Christian cross.

SERVES 4

4 cups all-purpose flour (480 g), plus more for rolling out dough

1/2 cup sugar (100 g)

2 teaspoons baking powder

Salt

Zest of 1 lemon

7 eggs

1/4 cup olive oil (60 ml)

1/4 cup milk (60 ml), lukewarm, plus more for wash

Sprinkles and icing, to decorate

In a large bowl or on a clean surface, combine flour, sugar, baking powder, and a pinch of salt. Stir in lemon zest and, using a fork, mix in 3 eggs, one at a time. Knead. Add olive oil and milk, and knead until you have a smooth ball of dough. Cover with a kitchen towel and let rest at room temperature 30 minutes.

Preheat oven to 350°F (180°C).

Place remaining 4 eggs in a saucepan and cover with cold water. Bring to a gentle boil. Reduce heat and simmer 9 minutes. Cool under running water and set aside, unpeeled.

On a lightly floured surface, roll dough into 3 ropes, each 1 to 2 inches thick, and braid them together. Cut into 4 pieces, each 10 inches long, and join the ends to create 4 donut-like shapes to surround each egg.

Cut 8 strips from remaining dough for decoration and set aside.

Transfer the 4 scarcelle to a baking sheet, placing an unpeeled hard-boiled egg in the middle of each. Form a cross over each egg with the reserved pastry strips. Brush with milk and decorate with sprinkles.

Bake at 350°F (180°C) for 40 minutes, or until cookies are golden brown. Transfer to a wire rack to cool.

Roll out remaining dough and cut with Easter-themed cookie cutters. Bake at 350°F (180°C) for 15 minutes, or until golden brown. Transfer to a wire rack to cool. Decorate with icing and sprinkles.

CASSATA SICILIANA

Though traditional to Sicily, this elaborately decorated dessert is known all over the world and mostly enjoyed on Easter, Christmas and other special occasions. Making a cassata at home is not difficult, but you do need to allow lots of time for the ricotta to rest and become firm enough to slice. This is a three-day-long endeavor, but please don't let this put you off. You just need to be organized. Here's how the three-day process unfolds: the first day the basics are prepared—the sponge cake and ricotta filling; on the second day the layers are assembled; and the third day is for frosting and decorating. The reward will definitely be worth the wait!

SERVES 8 TO 10

FOR THE SPONGE CAKE

Unsalted butter for coating pan

2/3 cup all-purpose flour (80 g), sifted, plus more for coating pan

6 large eggs (3 whole eggs and 3 yolks)

3/4 cup sugar (150 g)

1 teaspoon vanilla extract

Zest of 1 lemon

Zest of 1 orange

Salt

3/4 cup cornstarch (90 g), sifted

FOR THE FILLING

3 1/3 cups sheep's or cow's milk ricotta (800 g), well drained

1 1/4 cups sugar (300 g)

1 cup dark chocolate chips (175 g)

2/3 cup candied orange peel (100 g) (optional)

DAY 1: MAKE THE SPONGE CAKE AND FILLING

Preheat oven to 350°F (180°C).

Butter and flour a 9-inch (23-cm) cake pan.

Beat whole eggs, yolks, and sugar with an electric mixer on high speed until pale.

Add vanilla, lemon zest, orange zest, and a pinch of salt. Mix until batter becomes light and frothy and expands approximately four times the original volume. This ensures the eggs incorporate air, giving the sponge cake the desired volume.

In a separate bowl, combine 2/3 cup flour and cornstarch. Gradually add to the egg mixture in three stages, stirring gently with a wooden spoon or spatula. Use a slow, bottom-up motion to maintain an aerated mixture, being careful not to deflate the batter.

Pour batter into the prepared cake pan and bake at 350°F (180°C) for 35 minutes, or until golden. Check that a toothpick inserted near the center comes out clean. Let sit in pan 15 minutes. Transfer to a wire rack to cool.

To make the filling, place drained ricotta in a clean kitchen towel and squeeze to release excess liquid. Repeat 2 to 3 times until ricotta is completely dry, as wet ricotta will compromise the cassata's texture and structure. Push ricotta through a sieve into a large bowl. Add sugar and whisk until well combined. Stir in chocolate chips and/or optional candied orange peel, cover, and refrigerate.

FOR ASSEMBLY AND DECORATING

6 cups confectioners' sugar (750 g), plus more for dusting

Green marzipan or fondant (store-bought or see instructions on following page)

Candied fruit (oranges, citrons, pumpkin, cherries), to decorate

Royal icing (store-bought or see instructions on following page)

DAY 2: MAKE MARZIPAN AND ASSEMBLE THE CASSATA SICILIANA

Dust a 9 1/2-inch (24-cm) tart pan with confectioners' sugar.

Slice the prepared sponge cake horizontally to create three equal layers, each no more than 1/2-inch thick. These will serve as the bottom, top, and sides of the cassata.

Cut one layer of cake into strips the height of the tart pan. Then cut the strips into trapezoids.

Lightly dust work surface with confectioners' sugar and roll out marzipan 1/4-inch thick. Cut into trapezoids the same size as those of the cake.

Arrange alternating cake and marzipan trapezoids around the inside rim of the pan, creating a pattern where the top edge of one trapezoid fits snugly against the bottom of the other. Modify any edges and inaccuracies to ensure there are no unfilled spaces between each shape. You may need to trim the pieces for a good fit or add a small piece of sponge cake to ensure everything stays in place. This step is very important to help the cassata maintain its shape when you flip it onto a plate.

Trim the second layer of cake into a circle that fits the bottom of the pan and place it within the ring of trapezoids.

Add the prepared ricotta filling on top and level with a spatula to create a uniform layer.

Carefully trim the final layer of cake to completely cover the ricotta, ensuring a perfect fit within the cake and marzipan trapezoids. When the cassata is inverted onto a plate, this will be the bottom of the cassata, and we don't want any ricotta filling to escape.

Cover the cassata with plastic wrap and refrigerate 1 to 3 days. This resting time is crucial for the cassata to fully set and flavors to meld.

DAY 3: GLAZING AND FINAL TOUCHES

A cassata siciliana must be glazed several times and it takes a little patience.

For the glaze, stir 3 cups confectioners' sugar and 1 tablespoon water in a bowl. Continue to stir, adding a little water at a time until the glaze drips smoothly from the spoon.

Gently invert the refrigerated cassata onto a serving plate or cake stand. Please note that once you turn it out, you won't be able to transfer it again.

Place this plate on a tray or dish to collect the glaze drippings. Pour the glaze over the cassata and spread it over the top and sides with a knife. Clean the edges. Return the excess glaze to its bowl.

Refrigerate the cassata, uncovered, 30 minutes to set the glaze.

Remove and repeat, evenly applying more glaze on the top and sides. This time refrigerate uncovered 1 hour.

Place remaining 3 cups confectioners' sugar in a bowl. Add water as needed, but this time, create a much thicker glaze.

Pour the thick glaze in the center of the cassata to form a white disc on top. Using a spatula, spread it across the entire surface to create a smooth, even layer. Then apply one final layer evenly around the sides. Once this is done, place the cassata in the refrigerator until the glaze completely solidifies.

Arrange the candied fruit on top of the cassata.

Make royal icing according to package directions (or instructions below) and place in a piping bag. Using a small piping tip (Wilton No. 3), decorate the candied fruit and sides of the cassata.

Your cassata siciliana is now ready to be enjoyed!

You can purchase ready-made marzipan from specialty food stores and knead it with pistachio paste for an authentic Sicilian touch. If pistachio paste is unavailable, green food coloring can be used as a substitute, with a dusting of confectioners' sugar on your work surface. Or, to make your own marzipan, mix 1/3 cup sugar and a couple drops of green food coloring in a small bowl. Heat 1/3 cup water in a saucepan. Stir in green sugar until dissolved and it begins to boil. Remove from heat and mix in 3 cups almond flour. Transfer to work surface and knead 6 to 10 minutes until smooth. Sprinkle with confectioners' sugar if it starts to stick to surface. Form a ball, wrap in plastic, and refrigerate at least 3 hours before use.

To make your own royal icing, use an electric mixer to combine 1/2 cup confectioners' sugar, 1 egg white, and juice of 1 lemon. Whip on high speed to create a very dense white icing.

CANTUCCINI

Many recipes for *cantuccini* don't include butter, but I find it essential to achieve the signature crusty yet crumbly texture that makes them irresistible. Traditionally, these almond-studded biscuits are meant to be enjoyed with a glass of Vin Santo, a sweet "holy wine" believed to have originated in the fourteenth century. Today, this pairing remains an integral part of everyday life in Tuscany, where cantuccini and Vin Santo are almost inseparable, creating a warm and convivial end to a meal.

YIELD 2 DOZEN

1/4 cup (1/2 stick) unsalted butter (60 g), room temperature

1 1/2 cups sugar (250 g)

3 eggs

Salt

2 1/2 cups all-purpose flour (300 g), sifted

1 teaspoon baking powder

1/2 teaspoon nutmeg

1 1/2 cups raw almonds (200 g), whole

1 1/2 cups raw pistachios (200 g), whole

Preheat oven to 350°F (180°C).

Beat butter and sugar with an electric mixer until pale and creamy. Add eggs and a pinch of salt and mix until incorporated.

Add flour, baking powder, and nutmeg. Stir until a smooth dough forms. Mix in almonds and pistachios.

Turn dough out onto a floured surface. Divide the dough and roll into two logs. Transfer to a baking sheet lined with parchment paper. (It is a good idea to bake one log first to see how the dough behaves and how much it spreads.)

Bake for 15 to 20 minutes until lightly golden. Let rest 15 minutes on a cooling rack. Transfer to a cutting board, and while still warm, use a serrated knife to cut at an angle into 3/4-inch slices.

Return the sliced cantuccini to the baking sheet, cut-side down, and bake at 350°F (180°C) for 10 to 15 minutes. Keep a close eye on them so they don't burn. Repeat until all cantuccini are baked.

When cooled, enjoy with a glass of Vin Santo!

To give your *cantuccini* a beautiful shine, prepare an egg wash by whisking one egg white with 1/2 cup (50 g) of sugar until it becomes white and foamy. Use a pastry brush to generously coat the top of each unbaked dough log with the mixture before baking.

2,00
2,00
SUPER
PESCHE
EURO
2,50
EURO
2,50
Selezionati

summer

BRUSCHETTA

INSALATA DI POLPO E PATATE

ALICI FRITTE

PAPPA AL POMODORO

SPAGHETTI AL NERO DI SEPPIA

PASTA ALLA NORMA

SPAGHETTI ALLE VONGOLE

TROFIE CON PESTO ALLA GENOVESE

SPAGHETTI ALLA NERANO

LASAGNE

SPAGHETTI AL POMODORO ARROSTITO

POLIPETTI AFFOGATI

SPAGHETTI CON GAMBERI, AGLIO E PREZZEMOLO

TIMBALLO DI ANELLETTI ALLA SICILIANA

SPAGHETTI CON LE SARDE

PANZANELLA

MELANZANE ALLA PARMIGIANA

POLLO CON PEPERONI

CROSTATA CON FICHI FRESCHI

BOMBOLONI

TIRAMISÙ

GRANITA AL CAFFÈ

GRANITA AL LIMONE

CREMA FRITTA

BABÀ AL RUM

BRUSCHETTA

The correct pronunciation of this popular appetizer is *bru-sketta*, not *bru-shetta*.

This simple recipe captures all that is wonderful about Italian summers. There is nothing quite like the flavor of tomatoes grown in Italian soil under the scorching Italian sun. The ingredients are few, so we want to choose the very best of each.

The bread is the foundation of this recipe. Homemade sourdough and rustic Italian breads are best because they have a compact crumb and toast well, remaining lovely and crunchy yet absorbing the flavors of the topping. Toast the bread on both sides until golden, but still a little soft in the center—ideally on a hot grill. You can also use an oven, a nonstick pan on a stovetop, or a griddle. When you rub a raw garlic clove against the hot bread, the heat causes the garlic to dissolve onto the bread. Use tomatoes that are vine-ripened, red, and mature. Cut the tomatoes into small pieces. I like to use small Pachinos or cherry tomatoes. Each bite is a mouthful of summer!

SERVES . . . IT'S UP TO YOU!

Ripe tomatoes, chopped

Extra-virgin olive oil

Salt

Rustic bread, sliced 1/2-inch thick

Fresh basil leaves, hand-torn

Cloves garlic, whole and peeled

Freshly cracked black pepper, to serve

Place tomatoes in a large bowl with a generous splash of olive oil. Season to taste with salt. Stir well and refrigerate.

Just before serving, toast bread on both sides.

While bread is toasting, add some basil to the chilled tomatoes.

Rub a garlic clove over each slice of warm bread and then drizzle the bread with a little olive oil.

Spoon the tomatoes on top of the toasted bread.

Garnish each slice with a fresh basil leaf, season with freshly cracked black pepper (if desired), and serve immediately to prevent the tomatoes and their juice from making the bread too soggy and soft.

INSALATA DI POLPO E PATATE

OCTOPUS AND POTATO SALAD

Octopus and potato salad is enjoyed throughout Italy and not just in seaside towns. Light and delicious, it can be served as an appetizer or a second course.

SERVES 4

1 (2-pound) octopus (900 g), cleaned and trimmed

5 ribs celery

2 carrots

1/2 onion

1 bay leaf

Salt

4 potatoes, peeled and cut into chunks

Extra-virgin olive oil

1 red onion, thinly sliced

Juice of 1 lemon

1 bunch fresh flat-leaf parsley, chopped

Freshly cracked black pepper

Place whole octopus in a large saucepan and cover with cold water. Add 1 rib celery, 1 carrot, 1/2 onion, bay leaf, and salt to taste. Bring to a boil, reduce heat, cover, and simmer about 40 minutes, or until octopus is tender. Remove saucepan from heat and set aside. When completely cooled, drain, discard vegetables, and set octopus aside.

Bring a large pot of salted water to a boil. Add potatoes, reduce heat, and simmer about 20 minutes, or until soft. Drain potatoes and cover with a splash of olive oil.

Cut cooled octopus into 1/2-inch pieces and place in a large serving bowl.

Thinly slice remaining 4 ribs celery. Grate remaining carrot.

Add potatoes, sliced celery, grated carrot, and sliced red onion to the serving bowl and stir with the octopus. Season to taste with lemon juice, olive oil, lots of chopped parsley, salt, and pepper. Refrigerate until ready to serve.

ALICI FRITTE

FRIED ANCHOVIES

Fried anchovies are a common feature on many menus during the summer, especially at beachside restaurants. They're also a popular street food, known for being both delicious and inexpensive.

While some recipes call for simply dusting the fish with flour before frying, adding a crunchy breadcrumb coating elevates the dish. For extra texture, I use both traditional and panko breadcrumbs, creating a perfect balance of crispiness.

YIELD 2 DOZEN

24 fresh anchovies or sardines

1/2 cup rice flour (80 g)

1/2 cup all-purpose flour (60 g)

2 eggs, lightly beaten

1/4 cup milk (60 ml)

1 cup panko breadcrumbs (55 g)

1 cup dry breadcrumbs (120 g)

Peanut or vegetable oil, for frying

Salt

1 lemon, cut in wedges, to serve

Clean the fish. You can use a knife to cut off the head. But if you hold the anchovy in one hand and twist the head while pulling it away from the body, you will remove most of the intestines at the same time.

Butterfly the fish by slicing the belly from head to tail. Pull the vertebrae toward the tail, gently tugging the bone away from the flesh. Leave the tail attached and use scissors to detach the vertebrae at the bottom. This is how you keep the two filets intact. Rinse the fileted anchovies under cold running water, then place in a bowl of ice water.

Prepare 3 separate wide, shallow bowls or large plates. Mix the rice flour and all-purpose flour in one. In the second, mix 2 lightly beaten eggs with milk. In the third, combine the panko and dry breadcrumbs.

Dredge each anchovy in flour, shaking off any excess, dip in egg wash, and coat in breadcrumbs. Set aside on a tray about 15 minutes to let the coating set.

Heat oil in a skillet and test to see if it is ready by carefully dropping in a pinch of breadcrumbs. If they sizzle and float, the oil is ready. Fry the anchovies, 4 or 5 at a time, on each side until golden. Drain on paper towels.

Sprinkle with salt, garnish with lemon wedges, and serve immediately.

PAPPA AL POMODORO

Pappa al pomodoro, made from day-old rustic bread, is a perfect example of how Italians transform simple ingredients into something extraordinary, reflecting their resourcefulness and deep respect for avoiding food waste.

This traditional Tuscan dish has humble origins, relying on seasonal and accessible ingredients: stale bread, ripe tomatoes, garlic, basil, and extra-virgin olive oil. The height of summer is the ideal time to make it, as the market overflows with plump, juicy tomatoes at their peak.

Ask a Tuscan for the recipe and you'll find it varies by region, with each area adding its own unique twist. In Arezzo, for instance, onion is used instead of garlic, while some regions incorporate both. Regardless of the variations, the key to a great pappa al pomodoro lies in using the freshest, highest-quality ingredients. Whether served hot, lukewarm, or cold, it's always finished with a generous drizzle of extra-virgin olive oil, adding richness and depth to the dish.

SERVES 4

Extra-virgin olive oil

1 small onion, chopped

1 clove garlic, peeled and thinly sliced

2 pounds fresh tomatoes (900 g), peeled, seeded, and roughly chopped, or 1 (28-ounce) can crushed tomatoes (794 g), undrained

1 bunch fresh basil leaves, hand-torn

1 loaf day-old Tuscan bread, cut in 1 1/2-inch cubes

3 cups vegetable broth (720 ml) (see recipe on page 210)

Salt

Freshly cracked black pepper

Freshly grated Parmigiano Reggiano, to serve

Heat a generous splash of olive oil in a large saucepan over medium-high heat. Add onion and garlic and sauté 3 to 5 minutes, or until onion is translucent.

Add tomatoes and their juice and bring to a boil. Reduce to a simmer, add half the basil, and cover. Cook 20 to 25 minutes, stirring occasionally, until tomatoes begin to soften and break down.

Add bread cubes and broth. Let simmer until bread has absorbed as much liquid as possible and consistency is thick and hearty.

Stir in remaining basil. Season to taste with salt and pepper and let simmer 10 minutes.

Let rest about 1 hour. Serve in warmed soup bowls. Splash with extra-virgin olive oil, sprinkle with Parmigiano Reggiano, and garnish with basil.

Tuscan bread has been made without salt since a twelfth-century conflict in which Pisa severed supply lines to Florence. The cost of sea salt skyrocketed. In response, the resilient Florentines began making their bread without salt, a tradition that continues to this day.

SPAGHETTI AL NERO DI SEPPIA

SPAGHETTI IN SQUID INK

Spaghetti with squid ink might sound complicated, but it is really quite simple to prepare and very tasty. Though its origins can be traced to Sicily, the dish is widespread. From Venice to Calabria, frugal fishermen were expected to utilize every part of the fish they caught, including the ink from *seppia* (cuttlefish). The deep black ink lends a subtle seafood flavor to pastas and risottos.

If you are not comfortable cleaning a whole squid or cuttlefish yourself, ask them to take care of it at your seafood market. Let them know what you are planning to cook so they can give you the little ink sac. If it is tiny or if you are buying pre-cleaned squid, you may be able to find small packets of squid ink.

SERVES 4

Salt

1 (1-pound) squid or cuttlefish (455 g), cleaned and trimmed, with ink sac

1/4 cup extra-virgin olive oil (60 ml)

1/2 onion, finely chopped

1 clove garlic, peeled

Pepper

1/2 cup white wine (120 ml)

1 cup cherry tomatoes (150 g), cut in half

4 to 5 tablespoons tomato paste

1 pound spaghetti (455 g)

2 tablespoons fresh flat-leaf parsley, chopped

Bring a large pot of salted water to a boil.

Cut the tentacles from the squid and slice the hood into small strips.

Heat olive oil in a large pan over medium-low heat and cook onion and garlic clove until onion is translucent and just starting to turn golden. Remove garlic.

Increase the heat to medium-high and add sliced squid and tentacles (or grill the tentacles separately and use as a garnish). Season with salt and pepper. Add wine, stirring frequently until it has almost evaporated.

Stir in cherry tomatoes and tomato paste. Reduce heat, cover, and simmer 10 minutes.

Add squid ink by breaking the sac in the pan. Stir until ink is fully incorporated into the sauce. Cook 15 minutes, or until squid is tender and the sauce has thickened.

Add spaghetti to boiling water and cook 2 minutes less than package directions until al dente. Drain, reserving the pasta water.

Transfer drained pasta into the pan with the squid and continue to cook another 2 minutes to finish cooking the pasta. Add pasta water if the sauce seems too thick. Stir in chopped parsley. Ensure pasta is thoroughly coated in sauce.

PASTA ALLA NORMA

PASTA WITH EGGPLANT

It is said that when playwright Nino Martoglio tasted this dish in Catania, Sicily, in the late nineteenth century, he compared its excellence to Bellini's opera *Norma*, which is how this dish got its name.

Known for its rich culinary traditions and fertile land, Catania produces high-quality eggplants and tomatoes, making *pasta alla norma* particularly suitable for summer when these vegetables are at their best. It is traditionally served with *ricotta salata* (salted ricotta), which is also original to Sicily. This firm cheese is made from lightly salted sheep's milk curd that is pressed and aged for three months. It is perfect for grating and not overly salty.

SERVES 4

2 pounds eggplant (about 2 large; 900 g), unpeeled

Coarse salt

Olive oil

1 onion, finely chopped

1 clove garlic, peeled

1 (14-ounce) can crushed tomatoes (400 g), or 1 1/2 pounds ripe tomatoes (680 g), roughly chopped

Salt and pepper

1 bunch fresh basil leaves, hand-torn

1 pound mezze maniche or rigatoni pasta (455 g)

8 ounces ricotta salata (225 g), grated to serve

Wash eggplant and cut into 1 1/2-inch cubes. Place in a colander and sprinkle generously with coarse salt. Cover with a weighted plate to create pressure and extract the bitter liquid from eggplant. Set aside 1 hour.

While eggplant is resting, heat 1/4 cup olive oil in a large saucepan. Add onion and garlic clove and cook until onion is translucent and just starting to turn golden. Remove garlic clove.

Add tomatoes, salt and pepper to taste, and 2 basil leaves. Simmer over low heat 45 to 60 minutes, ensuring the sauce doesn't become too dry.

Rinse and dry eggplant on paper towels and place in a large saucepan or deep skillet. Cover in olive oil and fry until soft and slightly golden. Remove and drain on paper towels to absorb excess oil. Sprinkle with a pinch of salt.

Bring a large pot of salted water to a boil. Add pasta and cook 2 minutes less than package directions until al dente. Drain, reserving the pasta water.

Stir eggplant, some basil, and pasta into the tomato sauce until pasta is cooked. Add some reserved pasta water if needed to ensure pasta is thoroughly coated in sauce.

Garnish with grated salted ricotta and basil and serve.

SPAGHETTI ALLE VONGOLE

SPAGHETTI WITH CLAMS

Spaghetti with clams is, without a doubt, my favorite summer pasta. This simple but exquisite dish perfectly captures the essence of summer in Italy. It's a dish that instantly transports me to carefree summer holidays, where the sea breeze mingles with the aroma of freshly cooked seafood. The ideal setting? Imagine yourself sitting at an Italian beach club, a plate of spaghetti *alle vongole* before you, paired with a chilled glass of crisp white wine. A humble yet sublime celebration of summer's flavors.

SERVES 2

2 pounds vongole veraci, or baby clams (900 g)

Salt

6 tablespoons olive oil

2 cloves garlic, peeled and finely chopped

2 to 3 fresh red chili peppers, chopped

1/2 cup white wine (120 ml)

1/2 pound spaghetti (225 g)

1/4 cup fresh flat-leaf parsley (15 g), finely chopped

Bring a large pot of unsalted water to a boil.

Place clams in a bowl of salted water and let sit 20 to 60 minutes. Inspect and discard any clams that are broken or open. Scrub the shells clean, and rinse well under cold running water.

Heat olive oil in a large pan over medium-low heat. Add garlic and chili peppers. Cook gently, being careful not to burn the garlic.

Add clams and wine to the pan. Increase heat to high. Cover and cook about 5 minutes until clams open. Timing will depend on their size. Using tongs, remove clams, leaving the juice in the pan. Discard any unopened clams. Shuck half the clams, leaving half intact for serving. Set aside.

Add spaghetti to boiling water and cook half the time on the package directions.

Bring clam juice to a boil.

Drain spaghetti, reserving the pasta water. Add the very al dente spaghetti to the pan and stir with the clam juice until fully cooked. If it becomes too dry, gradually add small amounts of reserved pasta water. The starch from the pasta will help make the sauce creamier. Stir in reserved clams and chopped parsley.

Serve immediately with thick slices of Italian bread to mop up the delicious sauce or, as they say in Italy, *fare la scarpetta.*

Whenever possible, I buy clams on the same day I plan to cook them. In Italy, they're sometimes sold in bags of filtered seawater, which I keep them in until it's time to prepare the dish. If I need to purchase them a day in advance, I drain the clams while reserving the seawater. I then wrap the clams in a damp kitchen towel, place them in a bowl, and store them in the refrigerator. Before cooking, I soak the clams in the reserved seawater for at least 20 minutes to ensure they are free of sand.

TROFIE CON PESTO ALLA GENOVESE

Trofie pasta with pesto is a traditional dish from Liguria, but is known and appreciated throughout Italy. As in any simple recipe, it's important to use high-quality ingredients—especially when it comes to the basil, which must be fresh and fragrant. Trofie are a thin, elongated, and twisted pasta. The unique shape makes it perfect for capturing and holding the sauce, which is why it is favored in this recipe.

It is traditional to use a mortar and pestle to grind the ingredients for pesto, but for this recipe, we'll take the easier approach and use a food processor. Even though I have written quantities below, pesto is one of those recipes where you can play around, mix, taste, and adjust accordingly.

SERVES 4

Salt

3/4 cup extra-virgin olive oil (180 ml), plus more for preparation

1/2 cup pine nuts (65 g)

3/4 cup freshly grated Parmigiano Reggiano (75 g), plus more to serve

2 cloves garlic, peeled (optional)

6 to 7 cups fresh basil leaves, plus more to serve

1 pound trofie pasta (455 g)

Bring a large pot of salted water to a boil.

Heat a splash of olive oil in a pan over low heat and toast pine nuts 1 to 2 minutes, or until lightly golden brown. Keep a close eye on them as they burn quickly and easily. Let cool completely.

Place 3/4 cup grated Parmigiano Reggiano, pine nuts, and garlic, if desired, in a food processor or blender, and pulse until smooth. Add basil, and while the machine is running, add 3/4 cup olive oil in a steady stream. Taste and adjust seasoning as necessary, adding more olive oil if it seems too dry.

Add pasta to boiling water and cook according to the package directions. Drain and stir in the pesto.

Serve with freshly grated Parmigiano Reggiano and garnish with fresh basil.

SPAGHETTI ALLA NERANO

Spaghetti alla Nerano embodies the essence of Italian cuisine: simplicity, fresh ingredients, and a connection to local traditions and flavors. It is believed to date back to the 1950s and the small bay of Nerano on the Amalfi Coast. When restaurateur Maria Grazia needed to feed an unexpected large group of fishermen, necessity demanded she get creative with what ingredients she had on hand. Her ingenuity led to a dish that is now found throughout Naples and beyond.

SERVES 2

Extra-virgin olive oil

3 large zucchini, thinly sliced

1 bunch fresh basil, hand-torn

Salt

Freshly cracked black pepper

1/2 pound spaghetti (225 g)

1 clove garlic, peeled

8 ounces Provolone del Monaco or Provolone piccante (225 g), grated

Bring a few inches of olive oil to a boil in a pan. Fry zucchini in batches until golden. Drain on paper towels. While the zucchini is still hot, cover each batch with basil leaves, salt, and freshly cracked black pepper. The heat will release the flavor and aroma from the basil into the zucchini.

Bring a large pot of salted water to a boil and cook spaghetti 3 to 4 minutes less than package directions. It will be very al dente. Drain, reserving the pasta water.

Heat 1/4 cup olive oil in a large pan. Add whole garlic clove and remove when golden, being careful it doesn't burn. Add the fried zucchini and some fresh basil leaves to the pan.

Using a slotted spoon, transfer pasta to the pan with zucchini. Add 2 ladles pasta water. Finish cooking the pasta over a medium-high heat, stirring so the starch from the pasta creates a creamy sauce.

When pasta is cooked, remove the pan from the heat and add Provolone. Stir energetically until all the cheese has melted into a creamy sauce. Add a little more pasta water if necessary.

Sprinkle with some freshly cracked black pepper, garnish with basil, and serve immediately.

LASAGNE

If you asked most people around the world to name a popular Italian dish, lasagne would likely be mentioned just as often as spaghetti or pizza.

This recipe is a classic, traditional lasagne featuring a Bolognese meat sauce. Every family and every region has its own versions and opinions on how to make lasagne. Purists might argue that it should not contain basil, but I think it enhances the dish. Consider this a disclaimer to the many voices with strong opinions on the subject!

The key to making a truly delicious and memorable lasagne is to slow-cook the ragù for 2 to 3 hours. I suggest making the ragù the day before assembling and cooking the lasagne.

While you can make your own pasta sheets; for convenience, I will sometimes use fresh egg pasta sheets found in the refrigerator section of the supermarket. Leftover lasagne can be frozen and is also delicious reheated the following day.

SERVES 8

2 cups milk (480 ml)

10 whole black peppercorns

1 slice onion, 1/4-inch thick

1 bay leaf

5 tablespoons unsalted butter

2 1/2 tablespoons all-purpose flour

Salt

Freshly ground black pepper

Ragù (see Bolognese sauce recipe on page 22)

1 (16-ounce) box lasagne (455 g) or 10 to 12 fresh egg pasta sheets (see recipe on page 219)

3 cups freshly grated Parmigiano Reggiano (400 g)

1 bunch fresh basil

To make béchamel sauce, slowly heat milk, peppercorns, onion, and bay leaf in a small saucepan over low heat. When it comes to a simmer, remove from heat and strain, discarding everything but the infused milk.

Make a roux in a separate saucepan: Melt 3 tablespoons butter over medium heat, being careful it doesn't brown, then add flour and stir quickly to form a smooth, glossy paste.

Slowly add the infused milk to the roux, a little at a time, whisking well after each addition. Reduce heat to low and, whisking occasionally, let simmer 5 minutes, or until the sauce is thick and creamy. Season to taste with salt and pepper.

Preheat the oven to 340°F (170°C).

Coat the bottom of an ungreased 13x9-inch (33x23-cm) baking dish with a thin layer of ragù.

Arrange a single layer of pasta sheets on top of the ragù, ensuring they cover the dish. Cover with a thin coat of ragù, a little béchamel sauce, a sprinkling of Parmigiano Reggiano, and a few basil leaves.

Using the remaining ingredients, repeat layers of pasta, ragù, bechamel, Parmigiano Reggiano, and basil two to three more times, depending on the size of your dish. Finish with a layer of ragù topped with a generous covering of Parmigiano Reggiano. Dot sparingly with remaining 2 tablespoons butter.

Bake at 340°F (170°C) for 45 to 60 minutes, or until the top is golden and the sauce is bubbling around the edges.

Let rest 15 minutes before serving.

SPAGHETTI AL POMODORO ARROSTITO

ROASTED TOMATO PASTA

This is such an easy pasta to make, especially during summer when there are so many delicious varieties of tomatoes available. Make sure you use plenty of tomatoes—almost crowding them in the baking dish. And be generous with the olive oil. The only sauce your pasta will have comes from the tomatoes and oil and you don't want to end up with a dry and uninteresting pasta. This is another recipe where the quantities are merely a guideline.

SERVES 2

Salt

1 1/2 pounds cherry, Pachino, or Pisanello tomatoes (700 g), cut in half

2 cloves garlic, peeled and halved

Extra-virgin olive oil

1/2 pound spaghetti or linguine (225 g)

Freshly grated Parmigiano Reggiano or Pecorino Romano, to serve

Fresh basil, to serve

Preheat oven to 350°F (180°C) and bring a large pot of salted water to a boil.

Roast tomatoes and garlic in a baking dish with a generous splash of olive oil at 350°F (180°C) for 30 to 40 minutes, or until tomatoes release some of their juices and are tender, wrinkled, and starting to turn golden.

Add pasta to boiling water and cook according to package directions. Drain in a colander and transfer directly to the baking dish, stirring until pasta is thoroughly coated in roasted tomatoes.

Serve with a sprinkle of freshly grated cheese. Garnish with fresh basil.

POLIPETTI AFFOGATI

BABY OCTOPUS IN TOMATO SAUCE

Polipetti affogati translates to "drowned baby octopus" as the baby octopuses are "drowning" in tomato sauce. This wonderful recipe can be either eaten by itself as a *secondo* with chunky slices of Italian bread or stirred through pasta for a delicious *primo*.

SERVES 2

1 pound baby octopuses (455 g), cleaned

Extra-virgin olive oil

1 onion, finely chopped

1 clove garlic, peeled

Salt

1 bunch fresh flat-leaf parsley, roughly chopped

1/2 cup white wine (120 ml)

1 (14-ounce) can tomato pulp (400 g)

2 to 3 fresh red chili peppers

Pepper

Rustic bread or cooked pasta, to serve (optional)

Rinse baby octopuses in a colander under cold running water.

Heat 3 to 4 tablespoons olive oil in a pan and sauté onion and garlic until onion is translucent and just starting to turn golden.

Add octopuses, a little salt, and some parsley. Sear octopuses lightly and evenly about 10 minutes, or until they have curled up and released their juice.

Add wine and simmer until reduced by half. Then add tomato pulp and chilies.

Cook, covered, over low heat 40 to 60 minutes, or until octopuses are tender. The cooking time will vary depending on the size of the octopuses. Stir occasionally, and if the sauce seems too dry, add a ladle of boiling water.

Season to taste with salt and pepper. Sprinkle with remaining chopped parsley. Serve with rustic bread or mix with cooked pasta.

SPAGHETTI CON GAMBERI, AGLIO E PREZZEMOLO

SPAGHETTI WITH PRAWNS, GARLIC, AND PARSLEY

Spaghetti with Prawns, Garlic, and Parsley is the quintessential easy summer recipe, celebrating the fresh, vibrant flavors of seafood at its peak. This dish evokes the charm of an Italian trattoria by the seaside, where simplicity reigns and the day's catch is transformed into something unforgettable. With sweet prawns, fragrant garlic, and a hint of fresh parsley, this pasta is a true taste of summer—light, flavorful, and utterly satisfying.

SERVES 4

Salt

1 pound spaghetti (455 g)

1/4 cup (1/2 stick) unsalted butter (60 g)

1/4 cup extra-virgin olive oil (60 ml)

2 cloves garlic, peeled and minced

1 pound prawns or shrimp, peeled (455 g)

Freshly cracked black pepper

3/4 cup white wine (180 ml)

Juice of 1 lemon

1 bunch fresh flat-leaf parsley, chopped

Bring a large pot of salted water to a boil. Add spaghetti and cook 3 minutes less than the package directions. Drain, reserving the pasta water.

Place butter, olive oil, and minced garlic in a large pan over medium heat. When butter has melted, add prawns and season with salt and pepper. Cook until pink, 2 to 3 minutes per side, and transfer to a plate.

In the same pan, add wine and lemon juice. Simmer about 5 minutes.

Return prawns to the pan. Add some parsley. Stir in al dente spaghetti and cook 3 minutes. Add a little pasta water and mix well to thoroughly coat spaghetti in sauce.

Garnish with remaining parsley and serve.

TIMBALLO DI ANELLETTI ALLA SICILIANA

This baked dish requires some time to prepare, so please read the recipe thoroughly before starting. This way you can plan accordingly and enjoy the cooking process without feeling rushed or pressured.

As you may have guessed from its name, this dish is traditional to Palermo, where if you hear someone say *timballo*, they are probably talking about baked *anelletti alla palermitana*.

The recipe below is how timballo is typically prepared in Palermo, but you might come across many variations throughout Sicily—with salami, mortadella, prosciutto cotto, eggs, or slices of provolone or any other cheese that may be in the fridge. However, anelletti, a ring-shaped small pasta, is a signature element of this dish. Timballo di anelletti al forno alla palermitana is also a popular street food, prepared in individual portions.

SERVES 8

4 cups ragù (960 ml) (see Bolognese sauce recipe on page 22)

1 cup frozen peas (150 g)

4 large eggplants

Coarse salt

Extra-virgin olive oil

1 pound anelletti pasta (455 g)

1 1/2 cup dry breadcrumbs (180 g)

1 cup Pecorino Romano, tuma, or cacicavallo cheese (100 g), cut into small cubes

1/2 cup freshly grated Parmigiano Reggiano (50 g)

Make the ragù. While it is still hot stir in peas and set aside.

Cut 3 eggplants lengthwise into 1/8-inch-thick slices. Cut 1 eggplant into small cubes. Place all eggplant in a colander and sprinkle generously with coarse salt. Cover with a weighted plate to create pressure to extract the bitter liquid from eggplant. Set aside 1 hour. Then rinse under running water and pat dry.

Bring a large pot of salted water to a boil. Preheat oven to 350°F (180°C).

In a large pan, heat olive oil and fry the eggplant slices on both sides, in batches, until golden. Drain on paper towels. Repeat with cubed eggplant.

Add anelletti to boiling water and cook half the time stated on package directions. Drain and return to the pot. Stir in 2 cups of ragù to thoroughly coat the pasta.

Brush a 9-inch (23-cm) round pan with olive oil. Add breadcrumbs, shaking to coat the entire pan. Tip out the excess and set aside.

Line the pan with fried eggplant slices. Add half the pasta, followed by remaining 2 cups ragù. Scatter cubed eggplant and cheese on top. Cover with remaining pasta, pressing down to make it level and compact.

Sprinkle with reserved breadcrumbs, Parmigiano Reggiano, and olive oil. Bake at 350°F (180°C) for 30 minutes.

Let rest 2 to 3 minutes. Place a large serving plate on top of the pan, quickly flip it over, and serve.

SPAGHETTI CON LE SARDE

SPAGHETTI WITH SARDINES

The title of this recipe is a little misleading as I prefer to replace the sardines with anchovies and the spaghetti with bucatini. Yet it is inspired by one of my favorite, traditional Sicilian pastas, *spaghetti con le sarde*, spaghetti with sardines. The contrasting sweet and salty flavors from the currants and the fish are typical of the cuisine of Palermo. Though you can use sultanas, in Sicily they use *uvetta passolina*, which are small, dark currants.

I will confess that I rarely measure my ingredients when I make this, but instead throw in a handful of this and a generous pinch of that: *quanto basta!*

SERVES 2

3/4 pound fresh anchovies or sardines (340 g)

Salt

1/3 cup currants (50 g)

Olive oil

1 cup fresh breadcrumbs (100 g)

1/3 cup pine nuts (45 g)

5 anchovy filets in oil

1 small bunch wild fennel, chopped

1/2 pound bucatini or spaghetti (225 g)

Zest of 1 lemon, to serve (optional)

Clean the fresh fish. While holding the fish in one hand, twist and snap the head backward and away from the body, which will also remove most of the intestines. To butterfly the fish and keep the two filets attached, run your fingernail or scissors down the belly, from head to tail. Grab the spine at the end where the head was and pull toward the tail to gently remove the bone from the flesh. You can remove the tail as well, or you can leave it attached and use scissors to cut the spine off at the base. Rinse, pat dry, and set aside.

Bring a large pot of salted water to a boil.

Place currants in a small bowl, cover with hot water, and set aside.

Heat 1 to 2 tablespoons olive oil in a pan and toast breadcrumbs over medium heat, stirring frequently until golden brown, taking care not to burn them. Remove breadcrumbs and set aside.

In the same pan, toast pine nuts 1 to 2 minutes. Keep a close eye on them as they burn quickly and easily.

Heat a generous splash of olive oil in a large pan and cook preserved anchovies until they dissolve. Add fresh butterflied fish and most of the fennel, reserving some for garnish. Cook gently about 5 minutes until tender and flaky. Drain currants and add to the pan.

Meanwhile, add pasta to boiling water and cook 1 minute less than package directions. Drain and toss in the pan with the fish until thoroughly coated. Stir in half the pine nuts and most of the toasted breadcrumbs, reserving some for serving.

Divide pasta into serving bowls. Sprinkle with remaining pine nuts and breadcrumbs. Garnish with reserved fennel and, if desired, a generous amount of lemon zest.

PANZANELLA

BREAD AND TOMATO SALAD

Because it contains no artificial preservatives, rustic, homemade Italian bread is delicious the day it is made . . . and then not so great the next day. In peasant culture, wasting food was taboo. If, for some reason, bread needed to be thrown away, one would kiss the bread first—almost as if asking for forgiveness for such a wasteful act—a custom that continues to this day.

You'll want to use stale bread as fresh bread won't hold together when you mix in the dressing. Sourdough bread is probably your best choice, and if you don't have any that is stale, you can place sliced bread in the oven at a low temperature for about 10 minutes to remove the moisture.

Panzanella is a delicious summer bread salad and especially prevalent in Tuscany, though you will also find it in Umbria, Lazio, Marche, and Abruzzo. Like many dishes in Italy, each region has a different slant when it comes to ingredients and preparation. Some like to include tuna, mozzarella, cannellini beans, olives, capers, celery, and, more frequently, cucumber. You can get as creative as you like. In some locales the crust is removed from the bread. I prefer to leave it on for some added bite. Some cut the bread in chunky cubes, while others prefer it crumbled.

This is another one of those recipes where almost anything goes, and you don't need to follow weights and measures. I have added them as a guide, but I recommend just mixing the ingredients together and altering the seasoning to taste!

SERVES 4

1 medium red onion, chopped

1/4 cup red wine vinegar (60 ml)

1 pound ripe tomatoes (455 g)

3/4 cup extra-virgin olive oil (180 ml), plus more for preparation

Salt

1 loaf day-old Italian bread

1 bunch fresh basil

Pepper

Place onion in a bowl with 1 cup water and 1 tablespoon vinegar and let sit about 2 hours.

Chop tomatoes. If using a smaller variety such as grape or cherry, just cut them in half. Place in a bowl with a generous splash of olive oil. Season to taste with salt and let sit at least 30 minutes so juice is released.

Cut bread into chunky cubes. Transfer bread to a large serving bowl. Sprinkle with some water and vinegar from the chopped onion, ensuring bread is moist but not submerged in liquid.

Drain chopped onion and add to the serving bowl. Add tomatoes and basil leaves and mix well.

For the dressing, shake 3/4 cup olive oil and remaining 3 tablespoons vinegar in a jar. Season to taste with salt and pepper. Pour over the tomato and bread mixture. Using your hands to mix the ingredients is the most effective way of ensuring the bread absorbs the dressing.

Let rest at least 30 minutes and serve at room temperature.

MELANZANE ALLA PARMIGIANA

Eggplant parmigiana is a favorite in many homes in Italy, especially during the hot summer months. Once upon a time, it would have been brought to the beach in its baking dish for a family lunch under an umbrella.

Some people like to make this recipe a bit lighter by baking the eggplant slices instead of frying them, but if you have time, I suggest you stick to the original and traditional method. You can prepare this a day in advance and bake it just before serving. I often make more than I need and freeze it for later as it reheats so well.

SERVES 6

5 large eggplants, sliced 1/2-inch thick

Coarse salt

2 cups all-purpose flour (240 g)

Salt and pepper

Olive oil for frying

Peanut or vegetable oil for frying

8 cups tomato sauce (see recipe on page 213)

1 1/2 pounds fresh mozzarella (680 g), sliced

1 1/2 cups freshly grated Parmigiano Reggiano (150 g)

Fresh basil leaves, hand-torn

Rustic bread or cooked pasta, to serve (optional)

Preheat oven to 350°F (180°C).

Layer eggplant slices in a colander and sprinkle each layer with coarse salt. Cover with a weighted plate to create pressure and extract the bitter liquid from the eggplant. Set aside 1 hour. Then rinse under running water and pat dry.

Place flour in a shallow bowl and stir in some salt and pepper. Dredge each eggplant slice in flour, coating both sides.

Heat oil in a deep saucepan. I like to use an equal mix of olive oil and either peanut or vegetable oil. Fry eggplant in batches, turning once, until slightly golden. Add extra oil as needed. Drain fried slices very well on paper towels. (I usually use an entire roll!)

Coat the bottom of an ungreased baking dish with a thin layer of tomato sauce.

Place a single layer of eggplant on top of the sauce, keeping the slices close together. Follow with layers of mozzarella, sauce, a sprinkling of Parmigiano Reggiano, and some basil. Repeat layers two to three more times (depending on the size of your pan) using remaining ingredients and finishing with sauce, mozzarella, Parmigiano Reggiano, and some basil.

Bake at 350°F (180°C) for 45 minutes, or until all the cheese on top has melted and is golden and bubbly. Let sit 15 minutes before serving to prevent the layers from falling apart.

Serve with rustic bread or on top of pasta like my Aunty Nancy often did.

If possible, make the *sugo al pomodoro* (tomato sauce) the day before. The flavors will develop and it will taste even better. Any extra sauce can be served with pasta, used as a base for other recipes, or frozen for later.

POLLO CON PEPERONI

CHICKEN WITH PEPPERS

A staple of Roman cuisine, this dish is also known as *pollo alla romana*. Often enjoyed on special occasions, it embodies the communal and comforting aspects of Italian dining culture. It is traditional to serve this on Ferragosto, which always falls on August 15. The word Ferragosto can be traced back to 18 BCE with Feriae Augusti, a festival that honored the first Roman emperor, Augustus. As the Roman Empire converted to Christianity, this pagan holiday became a day to celebrate the Assumption of Mary and attend church. Later, Benito Mussolini declared the day a public holiday in part to create a national identity for Italy and encouraging the less wealthy social classes to use the opportunity to visit different parts of the country. To this day, August 15 marks the beginning of summer holidays in Italy. Many family-owned restaurants and shops close for an extended period as Italians head to the beaches, lakes, or mountains to escape the oppressive heat of the cities.

Pollo con peperoni is served hot at home, but is a favorite lunch during Ferragosto, traveling well for a delightful meal on the beach.

SERVES 4

2 to 3 bell peppers (traditionally red and yellow)

Olive oil

2 tablespoons unsalted butter

1 clove garlic, peeled

1 (3- to 4-pound) chicken (1.4 to 1.8 kg), cut up

1/2 cup white wine (120 ml)

1 cup canned tomato purée (240 ml)

1 tablespoon tomato paste

2 to 3 sprigs fresh thyme and/or basil leaves

Salt

Black pepper

Preheat oven to 350°F (180°C).

Remove stalks, seeds, ribs, and membranes from bell peppers. Cut peppers into wide strips and set aside.

Heat 1/4 cup olive oil and butter in a large Dutch oven or deep oven-safe pan. Sauté garlic 1 to 2 minutes, or until golden. Add chicken pieces and brown evenly on both sides. Add wine and simmer 2 to 4 minutes, or until it evaporates.

Stir in tomato purée, tomato paste, peppers, and herbs. Season to taste with salt and pepper.

Bake, covered, at 350°F (180°C) for 45 minutes.

Remove from oven and return the pan to the stovetop. Simmer uncovered over medium heat to reduce the sauce.

Many people cook this recipe completely on the stovetop. If you do, pay close attention to prevent the chicken from sticking to the bottom of the pan and burning.

CROSTATA CON FICHI FRESCHI

FRESH FIG TART

When I lived in Tuscany, our garden was graced with two beautiful fig trees. I'd head outside with a basket, intending to gather the sweet fruit to bring into the kitchen, but more often than not, the chore turned into a little feast beneath the tree. Figs are a true delight, and to me, the best way to enjoy them is fresh. This tart is a celebration of seasonal figs, combining a sweet pastry shell, creamy homemade custard, and ripe, sweet figs. It's a dessert reminiscent of the custard tarts adorned with fresh summer fruit you'll often find in pastry shop windows across Italy.

SERVES 8

FOR THE CUSTARD

4 egg yolks

1/3 cup sugar (80 g)

3 tablespoons flour (40 g)

1 3/4 cups whole milk (420 ml)

Zest of 1 lemon

FOR THE PASTRY

4 egg yolks

1 1/4 cups (2 1/2 sticks) unsalted butter, room temperature (285 g)

1 cup sugar (200 g)

1 teaspoon vanilla extract

Zest of 1 lemon

Salt

4 cups all-purpose flour (480 g), plus more for kneading dough

8 fresh figs, unpeeled and sliced

Make the custard for the filling well in advance so it has time to cool. Beat egg yolks, sugar, and flour together in a large bowl. Heat milk and lemon zest in a medium saucepan and bring to a boil. Remove from heat.

Whisk 1 ladle hot milk into egg yolk mixture. Repeat until all the milk is incorporated and transfer to the saucepan over medium heat. Bring to a boil, whisking continuously as the custard thickens. Remove from heat, place in a bowl, and cover with plastic wrap, letting the plastic touch the surface of the custard to keep a film from developing. Let cool to room temperature and refrigerate.

To make the pastry shell, in an electric mixer with a whisk attachment, beat egg yolks, butter, sugar, vanilla, lemon zest, and a pinch of salt until combined.

Replace the whisk attachment with the flat beater and stir in flour, a little at a time. Mix until flour is incorporated and you have a ball of dough.

On a lightly floured surface, quickly knead the dough and form into a disc. Cover and refrigerate a minimum of 4 hours, or preferably overnight.

Preheat oven to 350°F (180°C).

On a lightly floured surface, knead the prepared dough. Roll out to cover the bottom and sides of a 10-inch (25-cm) tart pan, trimming any excess to create a clean border.

Cover dough with parchment paper and ceramic pie weights. Bake for 15 minutes. Remove parchment paper and weights and return pan to oven. Bake for 10 minutes, or until the pastry is slightly golden.

Let cool completely and spread custard evenly onto the pastry.

Decoratively arrange fig slices on top and refrigerate until ready to serve.

BOMBOLONI

FILLED DOUGHNUTS

Bomboloni—filled, sugar-coated doughnuts—are a delightful treat commonly found on Italian beaches. Traditionally, men would walk along the shoreline with baskets filled with freshly made hot doughnuts. While this charming scene is less common today, you can still find beaches where children eagerly anticipate the call of "Bomboloni caldi!"—making these doughnuts a perfect afternoon snack after long swims with friends. During the summer, most beach towns today serve hot bomboloni as a late-night street food snack, filled with plain or pistachio custard, milk or white chocolate, hazelnut cream, or jam. Regardless of the time of day or your choice of filling, bomboloni are easy to make at home and are best enjoyed on the day they are cooked.

YIELD 1 DOZEN

1 1/2 cups milk (360 ml)

1 1/2 cups sugar (300 g)

1/4 cup (1/2 stick) unsalted butter (60 g)

1 1/2 teaspoons salt

2 packets (1/2 ounce) active dry yeast (14 g)

2 large eggs, lightly beaten

6 1/2 cups all-purpose flour (780 g), sifted, plus more for preparing dough

Peanut or vegetable oil for frying

Nutella, raspberry jam, strawberry jam, custard, and/or white chocolate, to fill

Add milk to a saucepan over low heat. Stir in 1/2 cup sugar, butter, and salt. Remove from heat when well blended and let cool to lukewarm.

Pour 1/2 cup warm water in a large bowl and sprinkle with yeast. Stir gently until yeast dissolves. Gradually stir in the lukewarm milk mixture.

Stir in lightly beaten eggs and flour to form a sticky dough. Turn dough out onto a lightly floured surface. Knead 6 to 8 minutes, or until smooth and elastic.

Place dough in a large, oiled bowl and cover with plastic wrap. Let rest 45 to 60 minutes, or until doubled in size.

Punch down dough and knead again on a lightly floured surface 2 to 3 minutes. Roll out dough 1/2-inch thick and let rest 2 minutes.

Using a floured 3- or 4-inch (8- or 10-cm) round cookie cutter, cut out multiple circles from the dough. Place on parchment paper, cover with a clean dry kitchen towel, and set aside to proof 30 minutes.

Prepare a plate covered with paper towels and a bowl filled with remaining 1 cup sugar.

Heat oil until it reaches 365°F (185°C). Fry each doughnut until golden and puffed, turning halfway through.

Drain doughnuts on paper towels. Quickly toss in bowl of sugar. Set aside and let cool before filling.

Spoon the filling into a piping bag fitted with a 5 mm tip. Insert the tip into the side of each doughnut and gently squeeze to fill.

TIRAMISÙ

The origins of tiramisù are rather contentious, with about five regions in Italy claiming it as their own. However, one thing everyone agrees on is just how delicious this perfect "pick-me-up" is! Every family has their own recipe and tends to be critical of any that differ. I confess I am no exception and believe mine strikes a perfect balance of ingredients and flavors. I learned to make the crema mascarpone from a pastry chef here in Italy, though I use a bit less sugar than he does.

Tiramisù is wonderfully versatile. It can be made a day or two ahead of time, which is ideal when preparing for large family gatherings. It shines whether served in one large bowl or baking tray, or as individual servings. If you run out of any ingredient, you can pause halfway through, refrigerate, and continue several hours later. It's especially fun to construct tableside and serve immediately. Adding alcohol is a personal choice. As long as it doesn't overpower the predominant flavor—which should be coffee—I find adding a tablespoon of liqueur enhances and complements the flavors of the dish.

SERVES 8

2 1/4 cups strong coffee (540 ml), preferably made with a moka pot

4 eggs, separated (4 whites and 4 yolks)*

Salt

1/2 cup sugar (100 g)

1 tablespoon Marsala, rum, Armagnac, or coffee liqueur

1 pound mascarpone (455 g)

1 (7-ounce) packet *savoiardi* (ladyfingers) (200 g)

Unsweetened cocoa powder, for dusting on top

Chocolate-covered coffee beans (optional)

**Consuming raw or undercooked eggs may increase the risk of foodborne illness, especially in individuals with weakened immune systems, elderly individuals, pregnant individuals and young children. Use pasteurized eggs if available.*

Make the coffee and set aside in a shallow bowl to cool completely.

Place 4 egg whites in the bowl of an electric mixer, add a pinch of salt, and whisk until soft peaks begin to form. Add 1/4 cup sugar and whisk until the sugar is incorporated and the mixture is aerated and glossy. Set aside.

In a large bowl, beat 4 egg yolks with remaining 1/4 cup sugar until pale and fluffy and sugar has dissolved. Add liqueur and slowly incorporate mascarpone.

Gently fold egg white mixture into yolk mixture a little at a time. Refrigerate if not using immediately.

To assemble tiramisù, dip savoiardi quickly in coffee and place close together in a single layer in a serving dish.

Cover with a layer of mascarpone cream and repeat layering coffee-dipped savoiardi and mascarpone, finishing with a layer of cream, until you are satisfied or have reached the top of the dish.

Dust with a generous sprinkling of cocoa and decorate with chocolate-covered coffee beans.

BIALETTI
Moka Express
MADE IN ITALY

GRANITA AL CAFFÈ

SERVES 2 GENEROUS PORTIONS

2 1/4 cups hot espresso coffee (540 ml)

1/4 cup sugar (50 g)

1/2 cup cream (120 ml), whipped and lightly sweetened with 1 teaspoon confectioners' sugar

Make coffee (a little stronger than how you would normally have it) and stir in sugar until dissolved.

Pour coffee into a freezer-proof bowl and set aside to cool. After it reaches room temperature, place in the freezer. Using a fork, stir vigorously every 30 minutes to break up any ice crystals that have formed. Repeat 2 to 3 times until the granita reaches the desired consistency.
Spoon a dollop of whipped cream into a serving glass. Using a fork, scrape the granita on top, and enjoy immediately.

You could also fill an ice-cube tray with the coffee. When you need a coffee granita, simply add the iced coffee cubes to a mini food processor, pulse a few times, and it's ready!

You can keep granita in the freezer for 15 days. (Not that it will last that long!)

GRANITA AL LIMONE

SERVES 2 TO 4

1 cup sugar (200 g)

2 cups lemon juice (480 ml), freshly squeezed, filtered (approximately 10 to 16 Sorrento lemons)

Heat sugar and 2 cups water in a saucepan. Stir until sugar has dissolved. Remove from heat and set aside to cool. When cooled, stir in lemon juice. Pour into a freezer-proof bowl and place in the freezer. Using a fork, stir vigorously every 30 minutes to break up any ice crystals that have formed. Repeat 2 to 3 times until the granita reaches the desired consistency.

If it freezes too solidly, break the ice coarsely and chop it finely in a food processor. Scrape into serving glasses, garnish with a slice of lemon, and serve immediately.

For a grown-up twist, try adding a splash of gin or vodka when you stir in the lemon juice.

Sicilian granita is a simple yet extraordinary treat made from just water, sugar, and lemon juice. A perfect balance between creamy ice cream and icy sorbet, its origins date back to Arab rule in Sicily, when *sherbet* or *sharbat*—a refreshing, fruit-infused drink—was introduced.

In the Middle Ages, *nivaroli* collected snow from Mount Etna and other mountains, storing it in *niviere*, stone-lined pits that preserved it for summer use. Some noble families even had private ravines to keep their snow from melting. In warmer months, the snow was grated and served with fruit syrups, a tradition that inspired Rome's *grattachecca romana*.

By the 16th century, Sicilians improved the process by using salt to lower the freezing point, developing the *pozzetto*, a wooden tub with a zinc bucket and crank. As the mixture of water, sugar, honey, lemon juice, or coffee was churned, it transformed into a smooth granita.

Today, Sicilian granita comes in flavors like lemon, almond, black mulberry, pistachio, chocolate, and coffee. Apart from lemon, most are served with whipped cream and, in true Sicilian tradition, enjoyed for breakfast with a soft, warm brioche—especially almond or coffee granita, the local favorites.

Simple ingredients, centuries of tradition, and pure Sicilian magic.

CREMA FRITTA

FRIED CUSTARD

Depending on where you are in Italy, you may find this delicious fried custard sold as street food or served as an appetizer, side dish, or dessert.

YIELD 20

- 4 eggs, separated (4 yolks and 4 whites)
- 2 cups sugar (400 g)
- 1/2 cup flour, sifted (70 g)
- 3 tablespoons cornstarch, sifted
- 2 cups whole milk (480 ml)
- Peel of 1 lemon
- 1 teaspoon vanilla extract or liquor of your choice
- Peanut or vegetable oil, for frying
- 2 cups breadcrumbs (240 g) (homemade with day-old bread placed in a food processor)
- 1/2 teaspoon ground cinnamon

Line an 8-inch (20-cm) square cake pan with plastic wrap.

Make the custard well in advance so it has time to set and cool in refrigerator.

In a medium bowl, beat egg yolks and 1/2 cup sugar together. Add flour and cornstarch and whisk by hand or with an electric mixer until pale and thick. If you feel it is too thick, you can add a little milk.

In a saucepan, heat milk and lemon peel until it's just about to boil.

Discard lemon peel. Whisk 1 ladle hot milk into egg yolk mixture. Repeat gradually until all the milk is fully incorporated, resulting in a smooth, creamy texture.

Strain through a fine sieve into a clean saucepan. Place over medium heat and whisk continually 10 minutes or until the custard thickens. Pour into the prepared pan and smooth with a spatula. Cover with plastic wrap and refrigerate a minimum of 3 hours or overnight until chilled and set.

Place flour, egg whites and breadcrumbs in 3 separate wide, shallow bowls or large plates. Combine remaining 1 1/2 cups sugar and cinnamon in a small bowl.

Heat oil to 300 degrees (150°C) in a saucepan or deep-fryer.

Turn out the custard on a clean surface and cut into small cubes.

Dredge each cube in flour, shaking off the excess. Then dip in egg whites. Finally, cover in breadcrumbs. Let rest 10 to 15 minutes.

Working in batches, fry the custard pieces until crisp and golden, turning only once. Remove with a slotted spoon and drain on paper towels. Dust with sugar-cinnamon mixture and serve hot.

BABÀ AL RUM

SERVES 15 TO 20

FOR THE BABÀ

1 tablespoon active dry yeast

2 tablespoons whole milk

3 1/4 cups bread flour* (400 g)

2 tablespoons sugar

8 eggs (cold from the refrigerator)*

2/3 cup (1 1/3 sticks) unsalted butter (150 g), cubed, room temperature

FOR THE RUM BATH

1 1/2 cups sugar (300 g)

Zest of 1 lemon

3/4 to 1 1/4 cups of rum (180 to 300 ml)

TO SERVE

Fresh whipped cream and strawberries, or custard and glacè cherries (optional)

**This recipe requires flour with a high gluten content and very cold eggs.*

In a small bowl, combine yeast, milk, and 2 tablespoons flour until a small ball of dough forms. Cover bowl with plastic wrap and set aside in a warm place for 30 minutes or until doubled in size.

Using a stand mixer fitted with the paddle attachment, mix remaining flour and risen yeast mixture on medium-low speed. Add sugar and eggs and mix for about 20 minutes until the dough becomes elastic and starts to come away from the side of the bowl.

Switch to the dough hook attachment. Gradually add butter on medium-low speed, waiting until each addition is fully incorporated before adding the next. Mix for about 15 minutes or until the dough is soft and smooth. Cover with plastic wrap and let rise at 80°F (25°C) for 2 to 3 hours, or until it has tripled in volume.

Preheat oven to 400°F (200°C). Grease the babà molds well with butter and flour or nonstick cooking spray. (For traditional babà, use individual molds just over 2 inches in height and 2 inches in diameter on top, slightly tapered towards the bottom.)

Gently deflate the dough with your hands.

With one hand, grab a portion of the dough roughly the size of the mold. Gently press it between your thumb and index finger, forming a small ball, and pinch it off as you squeeze. Wet your other hand, grab the ball of dough, and drop it directly into a greased babà mold. Continue until all the dough is used. Let the dough rest until it reaches the edge of the molds.

Arrange the molds on a baking tray, taking care to keep them separate, and bake at 400°F (200°C) for 20 to 25 minutes.

Remove from oven and let cool about 10 minutes before turning them out and letting them cool completely on a wire rack.

Stir 3 cups water (750ml), sugar, and lemon zest in a saucepan over medium heat. When sugar has dissolved and syrup is clear, turn off heat and add rum.

When the rum syrup has cooled to about 120°F (50°C), soak each babà for 1 minute, ensuring even coating. Gently squeeze once or twice to release excess liquid, then submerge again. After the final soak, avoid squeezing and place them on a wire rack set over a tray to drain.

Rum babàs can be served plain or decorated with freshly whipped cream and strawberries, or glacè cherries.

autumn

PORCINI TRIFOLATI CON PANCETTA

PORCINI FRITTI IMPANATI CON PARMIGIANO REGGIANO

ZUPPA DI CASTAGNE E FUNGHI

CANNELLONI VERDI RIPIENI DI RICOTTA E PROSCIUTTO COTTO

RISOTTO ALLA MILANESE

PAPPARDELLE CON FUNGHI PORCINI

CAPPELLETTI RICOTTA, NOCI E GORGONZOLA

PASTA E FAGIOLI

GNOCCHI DI ZUCCA

SALSICCIA CON POLENTA E UVA

QUAGLIE RIPIENE, PANCETTA E UVA

PEPOSO DELL'IMPRUNETA

BACCALÀ AL POMODORO CON OLIVE TAGGIASCHE E CAPPERI

BACCALÀ ALLA VICENTINA

POLENTA CREMOSA CON SALSICCE E FUNGHI

TORTA DI MELE

TORTA CAPRESE

SCHIACCIATA CON L'UVA

BUDINO AL CIOCCOLATO

SFINCI DI ZUCCA CON VINCOTTO

CASTAGNACCIO

FAVE DEI MORTI

GLI OCCHI DI SANTA LUCIA

CUCCÌA DI SANTA LUCIA

PORCINI TRIFOLATI CON PANCETTA

SAUTÉED PORCINI MUSHROOMS WITH PANCETTA

Noble, beautiful, and tasty, the porcino (*Boletus edulis*) has always been considered the king of mushrooms. It has a firm, compact, almost meaty flesh; an intense and pleasant aroma; and a delicate flavor. A versatile ingredient, porcini can be used in a pasta or risotto, sautéed and accompanied with toasted rustic bread, or eaten raw in a delicious salad. Porcini are a delicate ingredient and therefore don't require a lot of cooking, and this quick and easy recipe maximizes their flavor. Crispy pancetta is a perfect complement. You can eat this dish as is, serve atop toasted bread, stir through pasta, or enjoy as a side with any main course.

SERVES 2 TO 4

1 pound porcini mushrooms (455 g)

Olive oil

4 ounces pancetta or guanciale (100 g)

1 to 2 tablespoons unsalted butter

1 clove garlic, peeled and thinly sliced

2 tablespoons fresh flat-leaf parsley, chopped

Salt and pepper

Clean mushrooms using a knife to gently scrape the stems and the lower and upper parts of the caps to remove any soil. Wipe with a damp cloth and slice vertically.

Heat a splash of olive oil in a large, heavy pan. Add pancetta and fry until golden and crispy. Remove, drain on paper towels, and set aside.

Add 1 to 2 tablespoons butter and more olive oil, if needed, to the pan.

Add garlic and porcini and cook over high heat until mushrooms are golden.

Return pancetta to the pan with 1 tablespoon chopped parsley. Stir to combine. Season to taste with salt and pepper.

Garnish with remaining 1 tablespoon parsley and serve.

PORCINI FRITTI IMPANATI CON PARMIGIANO REGGIANO

FRIED PARMESAN-CRUMBED PORCINI MUSHROOMS

Porcini mushrooms are found in many regions of Italy. Their season varies from region to region and year to year, depending on the weather. Although you may find some in May or as late as July, the mushrooms during this period are smaller and not as flavorful as those harvested between late August and the end of October. Hiking through the woods and hunting for mushrooms is a popular weekend activity during the fall. Mushrooms tend to grow back in the same place each season and many people keep their favorite spots a closely guarded secret.

SERVES 2

2 large or 3 medium porcini mushrooms

2 cups flour (240 g)

2 eggs, lightly beaten

1 cup dry breadcrumbs (120 g)

1 cup freshly grated Parmigiano Reggiano (100 g)

2 tablespoons fresh flat-leaf parsley, finely chopped

Peanut or vegetable oil, for frying

Salt

Clean mushrooms using a knife to gently scrape the stems and the lower and upper parts of the caps to remove any soil. Wipe with a damp cloth and cut vertically into thick slices.

Prepare 3 separate wide, shallow bowls or large plates. Place flour in one. In the second, place 2 lightly beaten eggs. In the third, combine breadcrumbs, Parmigiano Reggiano, and parsley.

Dredge each mushroom slice in flour, dip in eggs, and coat in breadcrumb mixture.

Heat oil in a large, deep pan and fry mushrooms in batches, turning once, 1 to 2 minutes, or until golden on both sides. Remove and drain on paper towels.

Sprinkle with salt and serve immediately.

ZUPPA DI CASTAGNE E FUNGHI

CHESTNUT AND MUSHROOM SOUP

As autumn ushers in cooler evening temperatures, there is nothing more comforting than a bowl of soup. Celebrate with two of the season's most revered classic and traditional ingredients: chestnuts and mushrooms. Earthy tones and hints of sweetness create a perfect marriage of flavors.

SERVES 6

1 pound chestnuts (455 g)

1 1/2 cups dried porcini mushrooms (60 g)

1/2 cup dried golden chanterelle mushrooms (20 g), to serve

Olive oil

3 cups button mushrooms (225 g), chopped

1 large leek, chopped

5 to 6 cups chicken or vegetable broth (1.2 to 1.4 L) (see recipe on page 210)

5 sprigs fresh thyme leaves

Salt and pepper

Fresh dill, to serve

Using a sharp knife, slice a long slit across the top of the outer shell of each chestnut, being careful not to cut the kernel inside. Place chestnuts in a saucepan. Cover with water and boil 20 minutes. (Or roast on a baking sheet at 425°F (220°C) 30 minutes or until the skins split open.) Peel while still warm, removing both the outer shell and inner brown seed coat. Set aside 6 whole chestnuts for garnish.

Place dried porcini and chanterelle mushrooms in 2 separate bowls. Cover each with boiling water. Let sit 20 minutes to rehydrate. Drain in a fine sieve. Set aside.

Heat 2 to 3 tablespoons olive oil in a pan over medium heat. Add button mushrooms and leek, stirring often until mushrooms are soft and just beginning to turn golden. Be careful not to burn leek.

In a large pot, bring broth, sautéed button mushrooms and leek, rehydrated porcini, cooked chestnuts (remember to set aside 6 for garnish), and thyme leaves to a boil. Reduce heat and simmer about 20 minutes, stirring occasionally, adding extra broth if soup seems too thick.

Using an immersion blender, purée soup until you're happy with the consistency. Season to taste with salt and pepper.

Ladle into bowls. Crush the remaining chestnuts and sprinkle over each bowl; then drizzle with olive oil. Garnish with fresh dill and reserved, rehydrated chanterelle mushrooms.

CANNELLONI VERDI RIPIENI DI RICOTTA E PROSCIUTTO COTTO

SPINACH CANNELLONI FILLED WITH RICOTTA AND HAM

Cannelloni are tubular pasta shells traditionally filled with ricotta and spinach or a savory meat mixture. Similar to ravioli, they can be customized with your favorite fillings. In this recipe, I've used fresh spinach pasta and filled the cannelloni with ricotta cheese and ham (prosciutto cotto). They're cooked in a homemade tomato pasta sauce, or *sugo*, and finished with a generous topping of Parmigiano Reggiano, making them a true classic of Italian comfort food. While making pasta by hand is easier than you might think, you can always opt for store-bought cannelloni shells.

SERVES 4

Fresh 3 cups sheep's or cow's milk ricotta (750 g), well drained

1 1/2 cups freshly grated Parmigiano Reggiano (150 g)

1 egg

1 1/3 cups ham, finely chopped (200 g)

1 teaspoon nutmeg, freshly grated

Salt

5 to 6 cups tomato sauce (1.2 to 1.4 L) (see recipe on page 213)

Fresh spinach pasta (see recipe on page 220)

Flour for rolling out pasta

2 ounces mozzarella (60 g), roughly chopped

1 cup whole milk (240 ml)

Fresh basil leaves

Preheat oven to 350°F (180°C).

To make the filling, mix ricotta, 1/2 cup Parmigiano Reggiano, egg, ham, nutmeg, and a pinch of salt. Spoon into a piping bag and refrigerate until needed.

Place tomato sauce in a large baking dish.

Prepare thin sheets of spinach pasta (see instructions on page 216).

Lightly dust work surface with flour and lay out rolled pasta. Pipe a length of filling along the end of the sheet; you don't need a piping tip. Roll the pasta over the filling. Dampen the pasta edge with a little water to ensure it sticks, then roll it over again to form a tubular shape. Using a sharp knife, cut the first cannelloni from the sheet and place on top of tomato sauce in the baking dish.

Continue with remaining dough and filling. As you finish each cannelloni, arrange them side by side in one layer in the baking dish.

When the dish is full, sprinkle cannelloni with mozzarella and remaining 1 cup Parmigiano. Cover with milk and top with some basil leaves.

Bake at 350°F (180°C) for 35 to 45 minutes, or until the top is bubbling and golden brown.

If you have leftover pasta, filling, or cannelloni, there are plenty of ways to make the most of them. Extra pasta sheets can be cut into fettuccine, enjoyed immediately, or frozen for later. To freeze, dust the pasta with semolina, allow it to dry slightly, and wrap in individual portions. If you have extra filling, it can be used to make ravioli, which can be cooked right away or frozen for future use. Leftover cannelloni, whether cooked or uncooked, can also be frozen for later meals.

RISOTTO ALLA MILANESE

A recipe for *risotto alla milanese* first appeared in a cookbook in the early 1800s. Simple yet rich in flavor, it is relatively quick to make with just a few ingredients. In an ideal world, you would use saffron grown in Como, but obviously whatever saffron you can find will be fine.

Risotto alla milanese can be eaten as a *primo piatto*. However, the traditional recipe calls for ox marrow, which is why it is often served as an accompaniment to ossobuco. If you can't find ox bones, you can substitute beef bones. Ask your butcher to cut them in half for you. There are different options as to how you cook the bone marrow and incorporate it in the recipe. You can sauté it with the chopped onion as I do, stir it through the rice toward the end, or roast the bones and serve them alongside the risotto—scooping out the marrow to flavor each bite. Or you could do both! You can even eliminate the marrow altogether, but it would be a tiny step away from tradition.

SERVES 4

2 ounces ox or beef marrow (50 g) from approximately 1/2 pound halved bones (225 g)

1/2 cup (1 stick) unsalted butter (110 g)

1 medium onion, finely chopped

1 1/2 cups uncooked Carnaroli or Arborio rice (300 g)

2 tablespoons olive oil

1 cup dry white wine (240 ml)

2 1/2 quarts broth (2.5 L) (see recipe on page 211)

2 sachets saffron powder

1 1/2 teaspoon saffron threads

3/4 cup freshly grated Parmigiano Reggiano (75 g), plus more to serve

Heat bones, marrow-side down, in a pan over low heat until marrow softens. Scoop out marrow, break it up a little, and place in a large saucepan with 1 tablespoon butter. Add onion and sauté until translucent and slightly golden brown.

Add rice and 1 to 2 tablespoons olive oil. Stir with a wooden spoon and toast rice 2 to 3 minutes. Add wine and simmer 2 to 3 minutes, or until evaporated.

Meanwhile, bring broth to a boil in another saucepan. Reduce heat and keep hot. Transfer 1 ladle hot broth to a small bowl. Stir in saffron powder and set aside.

Add 1 ladle hot broth to rice and stir well over low heat. When rice seems dry, add more broth and continue like this, adding broth 1 ladle at a time. When you've added half the broth from the saucepan, stir in the reserved saffron-infused broth and the saffron threads. When that has been absorbed, resume adding remaining hot broth and stirring until rice is creamy and al dente. You may not need to use all the broth.

As soon as rice is al dente, turn off the heat and stir in Parmigiano Reggiano and remaining 7 tablespoons butter. Serve immediately while still hot.

Carnaroli rice is grown in Northern Italy's Po Valley. While you can use Arborio, Carnaroli has a higher starch content, which will make your risotto creamier.

PAPPARDELLE CON FUNGHI PORCINI

This recipe uses both fresh and dried porcini. I understand that finding fresh porcini mushrooms outside of Italy can be challenging. If you do come across them, be sure they are in good condition. Porcini are highly perishable and prone to pests. Choose mushrooms that are firm, with stems that are not soft or spongy. Also, check for small holes in the cap or stem, which could indicate pests.

I like to keep dried porcini in my pantry. Even when fresh are available, I like to add some of the dried porcini to my dishes as they have a more intense flavor.

Though fresh porcini are a delight as they melt in your mouth, this pasta will also be delicious with any other variety of fresh mushroom.

SERVES 4

Salt

2 cups dried porcini mushrooms (80 g)

3 tablespoons unsalted butter

1 medium onion, finely chopped

2 cups fresh porcini or button mushrooms (60 g), sliced

Olive oil

1/4 cup heavy cream (60 ml)

Freshly cracked black pepper

1 pound pappardelle pasta (455 g)

1 1/3 cups freshly grated Parmigiano Reggiano (130 g), plus more to serve

1 bunch fresh flat-leaf parsley, chopped, to serve

Bring a large pot of salted water to a boil.

Put dried porcini in a bowl and cover with 2 cups boiling water. Soak 20 to 30 minutes. Strain in a fine sieve, reserving water. Chop roughly and set aside.

Melt butter in a large pan and sauté onion over medium heat until translucent and just starting to brown. Add fresh mushrooms with a splash of olive oil and cook until golden.

Add rehydrated porcini to the pan and continue to cook 2 minutes. Stir in reserved porcini soaking water and simmer until half the liquid has evaporated. Stir in cream and simmer 2 to 3 minutes until the sauce thickens. Season to taste with salt and pepper.

Add pasta to boiling water and cook according to package directions until al dente. Using a slotted spoon, add directly to the mushroom sauce. Stir in Parmigiano Reggiano and mix well.

Sprinkle with Parmigiano Reggiano and parsley and serve immediately.

CAPPELLETTI RICOTTA, NOCI E GORGONZOLA

CAPPELLETTI WITH RICOTTA, WALNUTS, AND GORGONZOLA

If you like the strong flavor of gorgonzola and the earthy flavor of walnuts, you will love this pasta. *Cappelletti* means "little hats," a fitting name for this charming folded pasta.

SERVES 4

1 1/2 cups sheep's or cow's milk ricotta (375 g), well drained

1/2 cup freshly grated Parmigiano Reggiano (50 g), plus more to serve

2 cups walnuts (200 g)

Salt

Freshly cracked black pepper

1 portion fresh spinach pasta (see recipe on page 220)

Semolina, for dusting pasta

8 ounces gorgonzola cheese (225 g)

1/4 cup whole milk (60 ml)

1/2 cup fresh flat-leaf parsley (20 g), finely chopped

To make the filling, mix ricotta, 2 tablespoons Parmigiano Reggiano, and 1/2 cup finely chopped walnuts. Season to taste with salt and pepper. Refrigerate until needed.

Prepare thin sheets of spinach pasta (see page 220).

Lightly dust work surface with semolina and lay out rolled pasta. Cut circles of pasta with a 2 1/2-inch (6-cm) round cookie cutter.

Use a teaspoon or piping bag to add a modest portion of filling onto each pasta circle. Carefully brush the edges with a small amount of water. Fold each pasta circle in half, securing the edges firmly. Gently curl folded pasta, bringing the two tips together and pinch to ensure a secure seal. Dust with semolina and set aside on a tray lined with parchment paper.

Bring a large pot of heavily salted water to a boil.

To make the sauce, stir gorgonzola, remaining Parmigiano Reggiano, and half the milk in a pan over medium-low heat until cheese has melted. Add remaining 1 1/2 cups roughly chopped walnuts and parsley. Add more milk if you prefer a thinner sauce. The consistency is a matter of personal taste.

Place cappelletti in boiling water. Avoid stirring to prevent breakage and maintain a gentle boil 4 to 6 minutes, or until they float to the surface. Test readiness by sampling a piece retrieved with a slotted spoon. Ensure the edges are cooked.

Spoon sauce on serving plates and, using a slotted spoon, arrange cappelletti on top. Serve sprinkled with freshly grated Parmigiano Reggiano and cracked black pepper.

PASTA E FAGIOLI

Every Italian household has its own cherished recipe for *pasta e fagioli*, and each is a reflection of regional tastes and family traditions. The variations are endless, with no definitive right or wrong way to prepare it. Some versions include tomatoes for added richness, while others opt for a simpler, tomato-free approach. The choice of pasta is equally personal, ranging from long strands like broken tagliatelle to the rustic *maltagliati*—often made from leftover pasta scraps—or a short, ridged pasta like *ditalini rigati* from Gragnano, as shown on the opposite page.

SERVES 4

1 cup dried borlotti beans (200 g) or 1 (15-ounce) can (425 g), drained

2 quarts broth (2 L) (see recipe on page 211)

1 bay leaf

2 cloves garlic, peeled (1 whole, 1 finely chopped)

2 ounces guanciale or pancetta (50 g)

1/4 cup olive oil

1 onion, finely chopped

1 rib celery, finely chopped

1 carrot, finely chopped

2 tablespoons fresh flat-leaf parsley, chopped

1 sprig fresh rosemary

1 1/2 cups uncooked pasta, any shape (150 g)

Salt

Freshly cracked black pepper

Freshly grated Parmigiano Reggiano, to serve (optional)

Soak dried borlotti beans in a bowl of cold water a minimum of 8 hours or overnight.

Drain beans in a colander and place in a large saucepan with beef broth, bay leaf, and 1 whole garlic clove. Cover and simmer 2 hours over low heat.

Cut guanciale into strips and cook in a frying pan until golden and crispy. Remove cooked guanciale and set aside, leaving the fat in the pan.

Add 1/4 cup olive oil to same pan. Add finely chopped garlic, onion, celery, carrot, parsley, and rosemary and sauté until everything is slightly golden.

Drain half the beans, then blend them with 1 ladle cooking water. Alternatively, use an immersion blender directly in the saucepan to partially blend about half of the beans.

Add guanciale, sautéed onion, celery, and carrot to the saucepan and bring to a boil.

Add pasta and cook according to package directions. Season to taste with salt and pepper. Remove bay leaf.

Serve with freshly cracked black pepper and grated Parmigiano Reggiano.

Though borlotti beans are a staple in Italy, they can be harder to find in other countries. A great alternative is pinto beans, which offer a similar flavor and texture. You can also substitute cannellini or navy beans, both of which work well in their place.

GNOCCHI DI ZUCCA

PUMPKIN GNOCCHI

Nothing captures the essence of autumn quite like pumpkin, and this gnocchi offers a delightful twist on the classic potato version.

You may need to adjust the amount of flour based on the moisture content of your pumpkin purée. Take care not to add too much flour, as it can make the gnocchi less tender. Arrange any leftover gnocchi on a cutting board and place in the freezer for a few hours. Once frozen, transfer them to a plastic freezer bag. They can be cooked straight from frozen.

SERVES 6

FOR THE GNOCCHI

2 1/2 cups all-purpose flour (300 g)

1 (15-ounce) can pumpkin purée (425 g)

1 egg

3 tablespoons freshly grated Parmigiano Reggiano, plus more to serve

Salt

FOR THE SAUCE

1 1/2 cup (3 sticks) salted butter (340 g)

1 bunch fresh sage

3/4 cup pistachios (90 g), roughly chopped

Freshly cracked black pepper

Place 2 cups flour in a large bowl and add pumpkin purée, egg, Parmigiano Reggiano, and a pinch of salt.

Using a fork, mix all ingredients. Knead gently, gradually adding remaining flour as needed to form a soft but compact dough.

Shape dough into 3/4-inch-thick ropes. Dust generously with flour and cut into 1-inch pieces.

With a gnocchi board or the tines of a fork, roll each piece of dough to create ridges on one side and a hollow pocket on the other. (Or you can leave them as plain pillows if you prefer.) Place finished gnocchi on a well-floured board.

Bring a large pot of salted water to a boil.

Melt butter in a large pan and add sage and pistachios. Sauté until sage is crispy and butter is slightly brown.

Place gnocchi in boiling water 3 to 4 minutes, or until they rise to the surface. Using a slotted spoon, transfer to the pan with melted butter and toss until gnocchi are a little golden brown and "toasty" on at least one side.

Serve gnocchi in bowls. Spoon butter with pistachios and crispy sage leaves over the top. Finish with a generous sprinkle of freshly grated Parmigiano Reggiano and cracked black pepper.

To make fresh pumpkin purée, cut a peeled pumpkin into large wedges and remove seeds. Place pumpkin pulp on a baking sheet lined with parchment paper. Roast at 375°F (190°C) until very soft, about 40 minutes. Cooking time will depend on pumpkin size and variety. Let cool, then purée pumpkin in a food processor or a blender.

SALSICCIA CON POLENTA E UVA

SAUSAGE WITH POLENTA AND GRAPES

This delicious and satisfying second course can be prepared fairly quickly. While you can use any variety of sausage, I have chosen *luganega*, also known as *luganica*. This pork sausage from Northern Italy is long, narrow, and often curled into a spiral to cook in a round frying pan. When buying cornmeal, please read the instructions carefully, as some varieties are instant and require little cooking time. Polenta elevates any meal into the comfort food category.

SERVES 4

Salt

1 1/4 cups cornmeal (200 g)

1/2 cup whole milk (120 ml) (optional)

1/4 cup (1/2 stick) unsalted butter (60 g)

Pepper

Extra-virgin olive oil

2 to 3 bay leaves

1 long luganega sausage or 8 sausages (about 1 pound total) (455 g)

1 small bunch green grapes

1 small bunch red grapes

1 tablespoon fennel seeds

Bring 3 cups water and 1/2 tablespoon salt to a boil in a saucepan. Remove from heat and slowly pour in cornmeal, stirring thoroughly to prevent lumps. Return to heat and when it reaches a boil, reduce heat and simmer 40 to 50 minutes, stirring occasionally. If you like a thinner consistency, known as "wet" polenta, incorporate some milk until you reach your preferred texture. Stir in butter and season to taste with salt and pepper.

While the polenta simmers, you can cook the sausages on the stovetop or in the oven.

For stovetop cooking, heat a very light coating of olive oil in a pan over medium-low heat. Add bay leaves. Pierce sausage with a fork to prevent it from bursting. Cook about 15 minutes, turning often to brown evenly. Once the sausage is nearly cooked, add grapes and fennel seeds and simmer 10 to 15 minutes until grapes are plump and their skins have blistered. Discard bay leaves. Serve with polenta on the side.

If using the oven, preheat to 400°F (200°C). Spoon the polenta into a deep cast-iron pan, arrange the sausage and grapes on top, and bake 10 to 15 minutes, until the polenta is golden and crisped on top.

Before serving, drizzle with a touch of olive oil. For an impressive presentation to guests, consider placing the pan in the center of the table.

Traditional polenta, made from coarse cornmeal, typically takes 40 to 50 minutes of gentle cooking over low heat to reach a creamy consistency. If you're short on time, instant polenta—precooked and finely ground—can be ready in just 5 to 10 minutes.

QUAGLIE RIPIENE, PANCETTA E UVA

STUFFED QUAIL, PANCETTA, AND GRAPES

This delightful recipe combines the warm, autumnal flavors of sweet roasted grapes and salty, smoked pancetta. Although it calls for quail, you can easily substitute any game bird or even chicken for an equally delicious dish.

SERVES 2

2 Italian sausages, casings removed

1/2 cup fresh breadcrumbs (30 g)

1 egg

2 tablespoons whole milk

1/4 cup pistachios (30 g), roughly chopped, plus more to serve

1/4 cup currants (40 g)

Fresh thyme

Salt and pepper

2 bunches Concord grapes

4 quail

10 slices smoked pancetta or bacon

Olive oil

20 shallots, peeled and halved lengthwise

2 tablespoons vincotto or balsamic vinegar

Preheat oven to 350°F (180°C).

To make the stuffing, mix sausage meat, breadcrumbs, egg, milk, 1/4 cup pistachios, currants, 1 tablespoon fresh thyme leaves, and a little salt and pepper. Cut 10 grapes in half and add to the mixture.

Push stuffing inside the cavity of each quail. Arrange 4 pancetta slices over each breast and tie the legs together with butcher's twine.

Add 1/4 cup olive oil, shallots, 2 sprigs thyme, and just enough cold water to cover shallots to a pan over medium heat. After water has evaporated, reduce heat and keep on the stove until the shallots begin to caramelize. Be attentive so they don't burn. Add vincotto about 5 minutes before you think they will be done.

Heat a splash of olive oil in a large heavy pan over medium-high heat. When the pan is hot, add quail, turning to brown evenly, about 4 to 5 minutes.

Transfer quail and bunches of grapes to an ovenproof dish and bake at 350°F (180°C) for 15 minutes.

To serve, garnish with fresh thyme leaves and chopped pistachios.

Any leftover stuffing can be mixed with ground meat for a tasty hamburger.

PEPOSO DELL'IMPRUNETA

BEEF PEPPER STEW

The history of *peposo dell'impruneta* dates back to 1425, during the construction of one of Italy's most iconic landmarks, the Duomo in Florence. Architect Filippo Brunelleschi, already frustrated by numerous setbacks and delays, was particularly vexed by the time lost each day as workers descended from the dome's towering scaffolding to eat lunch in nearby taverns, only to face the long climb back up.

While visiting the kilns in nearby Impruneta, where the terracotta tiles for the cathedral's dome were made, Brunelleschi observed the workers cooking their lunches by slowly simmering inexpensive cuts of beef with red wine and black peppercorns in clay pots placed at the mouths of the kilns, where the bricks were baked. Recognizing a way to improve efficiency, Brunelleschi set up two canteens on the Duomo's scaffolding and arranged for orders of stew to be included with the tile deliveries. The stew was hoisted up to the workers, allowing them to eat without descending from the scaffolding. In doing so, the architect may have invented one of the world's first food delivery services.

Some modern recipes for peposo include tomatoes, though it's believed they weren't introduced to Italy until the mid-sixteenth century, following the discovery of the New World. Garlic, sage, and rosemary are also popular additions. While traditionally cooked in a Tuscan terracotta pot, a cast-iron pot that can endure hours of heat works just as well.

SERVES 4

1 1/2 pounds beef cheeks or beef muscle (680 g)

1 tablespoon whole black peppercorns

2 bay leaves

1 sprig fresh rosemary

Salt

2 cups Chianti red wine (480 ml), plus more as needed

2 to 3 tablespoons extra-virgin olive oil

Polenta, mashed potatoes, or cannellini beans, and Tuscan bread, to serve

Preheat oven to 325 degrees (160°C).

Cut beef into 2-inch cubes. Crush half the peppercorns with a mortar and pestle.

Put meat, crushed and whole peppercorns, bay leaves, rosemary and a pinch of salt in a Dutch oven or deep oven-safe skillet and add wine.

Cover and cook in preheated 325-degree oven 3 to 4 hours. Periodically check to ensure the liquid hasn't completely evaporated. If it appears dry, add more wine as needed.

Uncover and cook an additional 1 hour. The meat will have absorbed most of the wine and be very tender. The peppercorns should almost melt in your mouth.

Serve hot with either polenta, mashed potatoes or cannellini beans, accompanied by Tuscan bread toasted in the oven.

BACCALÀ AL POMODORO CON OLIVE TAGGIASCHE E CAPPERI

BACCALÀ WITH TOMATO, OLIVES, AND CAPERS

In most of Italy, fresh or frozen cod is called *stoccafisso* when air-dried, and *baccalà* when salt-preserved. Appreciated for its low cost and long shelf life, baccalà has saved thousands from famine.

Though you might find baccalà ready to cook, it is more common to buy it in its dried form. It needs 2 to 3 days to rehydrate, which obviously requires advance planning. You will often find the filets soaking in Italian kitchen sinks, especially on Fridays. I soak baccalà in a bowl of cold water in the refrigerator, replacing the water every 4 to 6 hours. When finished, the filets will be plump, tender, and ready to be transformed into a delicious meal.

SERVES 4

2 pounds salt cod filets, rehydrated (900 g) (begin to prepare 3 days prior; see directions above)

3/4 cup flour (90 g)

Extra-virgin olive oil

1 large white onion, thinly sliced

1/2 cup white wine (120 ml)

4 anchovy filets

1 1/2 (14-ounce) can crushed tomatoes (400 g)

1/4 cup Taggiasche olives (50 g)

2 tablespoons capers

1/2 teaspoon dried oregano (optional)

Salt and pepper

1 bunch fresh flat-leaf parsley, chopped, to serve

Preheat oven to 325°F (160°C).

Cut rehydrated cod into individual serving sizes and remove any bones with tweezers. Pat dry, leaving the skin on to help keep the filets intact during cooking.

Place flour in a wide, shallow bowl or large plate. Coat each filet well with flour.

Heat olive oil in a Dutch oven or deep oven-safe pan over medium-low heat and sauté onion, stirring occasionally until soft and translucent. Remove onion and set aside. Add more olive oil, and when hot, fry cod on each side until golden. Add wine and let reduce 1 to 2 minutes. Remove cod and set aside.

Place anchovies in the Dutch oven, stirring until they dissolve. Reduce heat and add canned tomatoes. Simmer 30 minutes. Add reserved onion, olives, capers, and, if desired, oregano. Season to taste with salt and pepper.

Place fried cod on top of the tomato sauce. Bake, covered, at 325°F (160°C) for 40 minutes. Alternatively, you can continue simmering on the stovetop, being careful that the fish doesn't stick to the bottom of the pan and burn.

Garnish with parsley and serve with hot rustic bread and roasted potatoes or cannellini beans. I promise you'll want to mop up any leftover sauce on the plate!

BACCALÀ ALLA VICENTINA

VENETIAN-STYLE BACCALÀ

Contrary to most of Italy, where the term *baccalà* refers to salt-preserved cod, in the northeast—including Veneto, Friuli-Venezia Giulia, Trentino—and parts of Liguria, it is used to describe air-dried cod, also known as stockfish.

For centuries it was necessary to beat stockfish vigorously to tenderize it and then let it soak in water for 3 to 4 days to remove the salt it is preserved in. I did this once . . . and I am happy to say that the stockfish we find in markets today is almost always sold ready to use.

SERVES 4

1 cup extra-virgin olive oil (240 ml)

2 large white onions, finely chopped

3 sardine filets, canned

1 bunch fresh flat-leaf parsley, chopped

2 pounds cod (900 g), skinned and deboned

Freshly cracked black pepper

1 cup flour (120 g)

1/4 cup freshly grated Parmigiano Reggiano (25 g), plus more to serve

1 cup whole milk (240 ml)

Grilled polenta, to serve (optional)

Preheat oven to 325°F (160°C).

Heat 1/4 cup olive oil in a pan and sauté onions until soft and translucent. Add sardines and 4 tablespoons parsley, and simmer about 50 minutes over very low heat until sardines have dissolved and onions are a golden amber.

Cut cod into pieces. Butterfly each piece, being careful not to cut all the way through as you will be folding the halves together.

Spread a small amount of onion mixture on half of each piece. (Make sure you reserve some to use later.) Season with a pinch of freshly cracked black pepper and close the fish together like a sandwich.

Place flour in a wide, shallow bowl or large plate. Lightly coat fish with flour.

Sprinkle half of the remaining onion mixture on the bottom of a Dutch oven or deep oven-safe pan. Place pieces of cod on top, vertically and snugly packed. Cover with the rest of the onion mixture and sprinkle with Parmigiano Reggiano.

Pour in milk and remaining 3/4 cup olive oil until cod is completely covered.

Cover, leaving the lid ajar to let steam escape, and bake at 325°F (160°C) for 3 1/2 to 4 hours. Do not disturb fish while it cooks.

Add some freshly chopped parsley and serve.

Rinse the salted sardines under cold water to remove surface salt, then soak them in cold water or milk for 30 minutes to 2 hours to reduce the saltiness. Then debone, clean and dry before use.

POLENTA CREMOSA CON SALSICCE E FUNGHI

POLENTA WITH SAUSAGES AND MUSHROOMS

SERVES 4 TO 6

Extra-virgin olive oil

1 medium onion, finely chopped

2 cloves garlic, peeled and quartered

6 to 8 Italian pork sausages (about 2 pounds) (900g)

1 (28-ounce) can tomato purée (794 g)

4 to 5 sprigs fresh thyme

Salt

Freshly cracked black pepper

3 cups button mushrooms (90 g)

2 cups Pioppini mushrooms (60 g), to serve

1 1/2 cups chicken broth (360 ml)

1 1/2 cups milk (360 ml)

1/2 cup polenta (80 g)

1/4 cup (1/2 stick) unsalted butter (60 g)

3/4 cup freshly grated Parmigiano Reggiano (75 g)

1 1/2 pounds baby spinach (680 g), rinsed and dried

Heat 1/4 cup olive oil in a large saucepan over low heat and sauté onion and garlic until soft and slightly browned.

Pierce sausages with a fork to prevent them from bursting. Add to pan, increasing heat to medium, and brown evenly. Add tomato purée and thyme, and season well with salt and pepper. When it reaches a boil, reduce heat to low, cover, and simmer 40 minutes.

Slice button mushrooms. Add a splash of olive oil to another pan and sauté button mushrooms over medium-low heat until golden. Transfer to a bowl and set aside. Cook Pioppini in the same pan until golden. Transfer to a second bowl and set aside.

Uncover the tomato sauce and simmer 20 minutes, or until it has thickened and reduced to a hearty consistency. Stir in sausages and reserved button mushrooms.

Prepare the polenta 20 minutes before you are ready to serve.

Bring broth and milk to a gentle simmer and whisk in polenta and salt. Reduce heat to very low and cook about 20 minutes, whisking frequently. Add butter and freshly grated Parmigiano Reggiano, and continue whisking until butter has melted and the polenta is smooth and creamy.

Sauté baby spinach in a pan over medium heat, stirring gently until the leaves are wilted. You don't need to add oil as the water content in the spinach will prevent it from sticking to the pan. This will only take a couple of minutes, and the spinach should be a lovely bright green.

To serve, place a generous spoonful of polenta in the center of each plate. Top with sausages (sliced, if desired) and sauce, with reserved Pioppini and spinach on the side. Drizzle with olive oil and a sprinkle of freshly cracked black pepper.

A perfect recipe for cold autumn evenings or a cozy Sunday family lunch with loved ones.

TORTA DI MELE

APPLE CAKE

For this cake, feel free to use any type of apple you like. Having said that, I prefer Granny Smiths when I bake.

SERVES 8

1 tablespoon unsalted butter

3 apples, peeled and cored

Juice and zest of 1 lemon

3/4 cup sugar (150 g)

2 large eggs

1/2 cup milk (120 ml)

1/3 cup sunflower oil (80 ml)

2 cups self-rising flour* (240 g), plus more for preparation

1/3 cup potato starch (45 g)

1/2 teaspoon ground cinnamon

Confectioners' sugar and vanilla gelato, to serve

**If using all-purpose flour, mix 2 cups of flour with 1 tablespoon baking powder and 1/2 teaspoon salt.*

Preheat oven to 350°F (180°C).

Butter and line a 9-inch (23-cm) cake pan with parchment paper.

Cut 2 apples into small cubes. Place in a bowl and sprinkle with lemon juice to prevent browning. Set aside.

Beat sugar, eggs, and lemon zest with an electric mixer until pale and frothy and increased in volume. Slowly mix in milk and oil.

Sift flour, potato starch, and cinnamon together and stir into the wet mixture until combined.

Lightly sprinkle the cubed apples with flour to keep them from sinking to the bottom of the cake. Fold into batter.

Pour batter into the prepared pan. Cut remaining apple into very thin slices and arrange on the surface, either flat or on their sides slightly sunk into the batter.

Bake at 350°F (180°C) for 55 to 60 minutes, or until a toothpick comes out clean. Cool in pan 10 minutes. Then gently turn out on a wire rack.

Dust with confectioners' sugar and serve with a large scoop of vanilla gelato!

TORTA CAPRESE

FLOURLESS ALMOND AND CHOCOLATE CAKE

Moist on the inside with a lovely crust, this flourless Neapolitan dessert melts in your mouth with every bite. If you've never had torta caprese, it's like an Italian version of a rich chocolate brownie.

SERVES 12

9 ounces dark chocolate (255 g), cut in small pieces

1 cup (2 sticks) unsalted butter (225 g), room temperature, plus more for coating pan

1 cup sugar (200 g)

5 eggs, separated (5 yolks and 5 whites)

3 cups almond flour (300 g)

1 cup (150g whole almonds), roughly chopped

1 tablespoon orange liqueur or rum (optional)

Confectioners' sugar, to serve

Preheat oven to 350°F (175°C)

Melt chocolate *a bagnomaria* (in a heatproof bowl set over a saucepan of simmering water) or use a microwave. Set aside.

Generously butter the bottom and sides of an 11-inch (28-cm) cake pan. Line the bottom with parchment paper.

Set aside 3 tablespoons sugar.

Using a stand mixer fitted with the paddle attachment, mix butter and remaining sugar on high speed 5 minutes, or until pale, light, and fluffy.

Add egg yolks, one at a time, and beat 3 to 4 minutes until well combined.

Mix in cooled melted chocolate on medium speed. Add almond flour and mix to combine. Stir in chopped almonds.

In a separate bowl, beat egg whites with reserved 3 tablespoons sugar until stiff peaks form.

Gently fold egg white mixture into the chocolate mixture from the bottom to the top, ensuring you don't lose the air you have whisked into both.

Pour batter into the prepared cake pan and level the surface with a spatula.

Bake at 350°F (180°C) for 35 to 40 minutes or until an inserted skewer comes out clean.

Let cake sit about 30 minutes before turning out on a wire rack to cool completely. Slice the Torta Caprese cold.

Generously sprinkle with confectioners' sugar before serving.

SCHIACCIATA CON L'UVA

TUSCAN GRAPE FOCACCIA

If you happen to be in Tuscany during autumn *vendemmia*—the grape harvest—you will see *schiacciata con l'uva* in the windows of most bakeries. Please make sure you buy a big slice!

I like to use *uva fragola*, a small black wine grape that we can find in Italy, but you can substitute Concord grapes.

SERVES 8

Extra-virgin olive oil

3 cups all-purpose flour (360 g), plus more for rolling out dough

3 packets (3/4 ounce) active dry yeast (21 g)

1 cup sugar (200 g)

Salt

2 pounds black wine grapes (900 g), seeds removed if necessary

Fresh rosemary, roughly chopped (optional)

Preheat oven to 360°F (180°C).

Lightly coat a large bowl with olive oil.

In another bowl, combine flour, yeast, 2 tablespoons sugar, a pinch of salt, 2 tablespoons olive oil, and about 1/2 cup warm water. Knead, adding more water as needed until dough is compact and pulls away from the bowl. Remove and continue kneading on a lightly floured surface 5 to 10 minutes, or until smooth. Place in oiled bowl and cover with a kitchen towel. Let rise at least 1 hour.

On a lightly floured surface, roll out half the dough. Place in baking tray or round cake pan, pushing to spread the dough to the edges of the form.

Scatter half of the grapes over the dough and sprinkle with 2 to 3 tablespoons sugar.

Roll out remaining dough, place on top of grapes and press lightly until you feel the grapes pop a little between the dough. Place remaining grapes on top. Sprinkle with 2 to 3 tablespoons sugar and fresh rosemary, if desired. You may have sugar left over.

Drizzle a little olive oil on top, then use a pastry brush to spread it evenly. Make sure the oil covers the surface completely and reaches the edges, as this will help prevent sticking.

Bake at 360°F (180°C) for about 30 minutes, or until golden.

This dessert is best served warm from the oven.

BUDINO AL CIOCCOLATO

CHOCOLATE PUDDING

Chocolate pudding is the ultimate comfort food, bringing back cherished childhood memories with every spoonful. Its rich, velvety texture and deep chocolate flavor make it a simple yet indulgent timeless classic. To get the best result, use good quality dark chocolate.

SERVES 6

3 ounces dark chocolate (85 g)

1/4 cup (1/2 stick) unsalted butter (60 g), room temperature

1/3 cup sugar (80 g)

1 egg

3/4 cup cornstarch (90 g)

4 tablespoons unsweetened cocoa powder

4 1/2 cups whole milk (1 L)

Melt chocolate *a bagnomaria* (in a heatproof bowl set over a saucepan of simmering water) or use a microwave. Set aside and let cool.

Beat butter and sugar with an electric mixer until pale and creamy.

Add egg and mix until incorporated. Stir in cornstarch, cocoa, and cooled melted chocolate.

Transfer to a saucepan. Add milk and whisk over medium-high heat until boiling. Continue whisking at a gentle boil 2 minutes.

Pour into individual serving bowls or one large bowl. Bring to room temperature and refrigerate a minimum of 6 hours, or preferably overnight.

SFINCI DI ZUCCA CON VINCOTTO

PUMPKIN DOUGHNUTS WITH VINCOTTO

YIELD 2 DOZEN

1/3 cup currants, raisins, or sultanas (50 g)

1/2 cup port (120 ml)

2 cups sugar (400 g)

1 teaspoon ground cinnamon

1 pumpkin (approximately 2 pounds) (900 g), peeled, seeded, and cubed or 1 (15-ounce) can pumpkin purée (425 g)

1 ounce fresh brewer's yeast (28 g)

1 cup whole milk (240 ml), lukewarm

2 1/2 cups all-purpose flour (450 g)

Salt

1 tablespoon fresh rosemary, chopped

Peanut or vegetable oil for frying

Vincotto glaze (see note)

Soak currants in port 30 minutes, or until plump.

Combine sugar and cinnamon and set aside.

If using fresh pumpkin, place in a saucepan, cover with water, and bring to a boil. Reduce heat and simmer until pumpkin is soft. Drain and purée in a food processor or blender. Let cool.

Dissolve yeast in lukewarm milk.

Sift flour into a large bowl, add a pinch of salt, and make a well in the center.

Slowly add milk and dissolved yeast, stirring with a fork to incorporate flour and milk.

Strain currants and add to dough. Stir in pumpkin and rosemary until dough is uniform in consistency and color.

Cover with a kitchen towel and place in a warm spot to rise 2 hours until doubled in size.

Heat oil to 350°F (180°C) in a deep saucepan or deep fryer. Scoop a spoonful of dough, and with another spoon, push the dough into the oil. Repeat and cook about 5 *sfinci* at a time, turning until golden. Drain on paper towels.

Roll the warm sfinci in the sugar and cinnamon mixture.

Drizzle with *vincotto* glaze just before serving. Serve warm, if possible, though sfinci really are delicious at any temperature.

To make your own vincotto glaze, place 3 1/2 cups fruity red wine, 3/4 cup sugar, 1-inch piece peeled fresh ginger (cut in thirds), 1 stick cinnamon, 1 teaspoon cardamom pods, and 2 cloves in a saucepan and bring to a boil. Reduce heat to medium and simmer about 30 minutes until thickened and reduced to about 3/4 cup of syrup. Strain through a sieve and let cool to room temperature.

CASTAGNACCIO

CHESTNUT FLOUR CAKE

Castagnaccio exemplifies the resourcefulness of *cucina povera*, or peasant cooking, where local, seasonal, and humble ingredients are transformed into delightful dishes that have endured for centuries. You will find this cake in Veneto, Piedmont, Lombardy, and wherever chestnuts grow.

SERVES 8

1/2 cup raisins (80 g), plus more to serve

4 tablespoons olive oil, plus more for coating pan

4 cups chestnut flour (400 g)

1/4 cup sugar (50 g)

Salt

1/2 cup pine nuts (65 g), plus more to serve

1 sprig fresh rosemary, roughly chopped

Preheat oven to 400°F (200°C).

Soak raisins in warm water 20 minutes, or until plump.

Coat the bottom and sides of a 12x9-inch (30x23-cm) cake pan with olive oil.

Stir chestnut flour, sugar, and a pinch of salt in a large bowl. Add 4 tablespoons olive oil and about 3 1/2 cups cold water, a little at a time, stirring constantly to obtain a smooth mixture without lumps.

Pour into the prepared pan and sprinkle with strained raisins, pine nuts, and rosemary.

Bake at 400°F (200°C) for about 50 minutes, or until golden.

Serve warm and sprinkle with raisins and pine nuts, if desired.

FAVE DEI MORTI

ALMOND COOKIES TO CELEBRATE THE FEAST OF ALL SOULS

Festa dei morti—Day of the Dead—is a solemn Italian and Christian holiday dedicated to praying for the souls of deceased loved ones. Observed on November 2, the day after All Saints' Day, this tradition dates back to the tenth century. Throughout Italy, the Feast of the Dead includes various sweets—typically dry—such as *fanfalucchie* in Lecce, *pane dei santi* in Siena, *ossi di morti* in Sicily, and *pan dei morti* in Lombardy.

Fave dei morti are found in bakeries and pastry shops in northern and central Italy. Despite the absence of beans in the recipe, the name translates to "beans of the dead." In ancient Rome, broad beans symbolized the souls of the dead, and this legume was offered as a gift to the gods of Hades. Numerous superstitious rituals involved chewing dried broad beans, cooking them, or offering them as donations to the tombs of the deceased.

Christianity and peasant traditions have preserved the link between broad beans and the dead. Even in modern times, one might see bowls full of broad beans and other legumes on street corners or windowsills in early November. In more recent times, fave dei morti were traditionally sold at cemetery entrances, allowing people to honor the deceased with these symbolic treats.

YIELD 2 DOZEN

2 cups almonds (280 g) or almond flour (200 g)

3/4 cup 00 flour (90 g)

1/2 cup sugar (100 g)

1 egg

2 tablespoons unsalted butter, melted

Zest of 1 lemon or ground cinnamon

1 to 2 tablespoons rum (optional)

Preheat oven to 350°F (180°C).

If using whole almonds, pulse them in a food processor just until they become a fine flour. Be careful not to overprocess them, as this can cause almonds to release their oils.

Mix almond flour, 00 flour, and sugar in a bowl. Make a well in the center and add egg, butter, and lemon zest or a pinch of cinnamon, and knead into a soft and compact dough. If the dough seems dry, add 1 to 2 tablespoons rum or water.

Using a tablespoon as a measure, scoop out pieces of dough and roll them into balls. Lightly flatten each ball with the back of a spoon or your thumb.

Arrange on baking tray and bake at 350°F (180°C) for 15 minutes, or until slightly golden.

Cool on wire rack.

Enjoy with a cup of tea or coffee, but for a truly perfect pairing, savor them with a glass of good Vin Santo!

GLI OCCHI DI SANTA LUCIA

December 13 marks the feast of Saint Lucia, the patron saint of the blind and those suffering from eye ailments. Saint Lucia, a third-century martyr from Syracuse, Sicily, is associated with vision due to legends of her being tortured and having her eyes gouged out, only for her sight to be miraculously restored. This led to her patronage over vision-related issues.

In the region of Puglia, particularly Bari, *gli occhi di* Santa Lucia ("the eyes of Santa Lucia") are traditional sweets, similar in shape to the savory *taralli* from the same area. When making these cookies, it is best to use light extra-virgin olive oil and quality white wine. Be careful not to overcook them; they should remain pale, so take them out of the oven as soon as they turn slightly golden.

YIELD 3 DOZEN

4 cups all-purpose flour (480 g), sifted

1 tablespoon sugar

1/2 cup olive oil (120 ml)

1/2 cup white wine (120 ml)

2 1/2 cups confectioners' sugar (300 g), sifted

Preheat oven to 325°F (160°C).

Stir flour, sugar, olive oil, and wine in a large bowl and knead by hand into a compact and elastic dough.

Roll dough into ropes, then bring the ends together and pinch firmly to form individual rings.

Arrange on a baking sheet lined with parchment paper and bake at 325°F (160°C) for 30 minutes. Remove from oven and let cool completely.

Place confectioners' sugar in a bowl and stir in hot water, a little at a time, until you get a smooth and thick glaze. Dip each cookie in the glaze and place on a wire rack.

CUCCÌA DI SANTA LUCIA

Cuccìa di Santa Lucia is a traditional Sicilian dessert prepared to commemorate Saint Lucia's feast day on December 13, the anniversary of her death in 304 AD.

Its origins date back to a three-year famine in Syracuse, Sicily, in the mid-1700s. Desperate for relief, the devout villagers prayed to their patron saint, Saint Lucia, for her intercession. According to legend, on December 13, their prayers were answered when a ship loaded with wheat arrived at the port. Overcome with hunger, they cooked the grain immediately without grinding it into flour for bread or pasta.

To this day, bread and pasta are not consumed on this holiday. The preparation of cuccìa for Santa Lucia is a cherished ritual in Sicilian families that begins two or three days before the holiday. The wheat grains are rinsed and soaked in cold water, which is changed daily. On December 12, the grains are immersed in water and cooked in a large pot until tender, which can take up to three hours. Once swollen and soft, the grains are left to cool in the cooking water before being drained.

In Italy, *grano cotto*, precooked wheat, is available in most supermarkets. If you cannot find it at a specialty market or online, you will need to soak wheat berries using the traditional method.

SERVES 4

3 1/2 cups sheep's or cow's milk ricotta, well drained (800 g)

3/4 cup sugar (150 g)

1 teaspoon vanilla extract

1 cup candied fruit, orange peel and cherries (155 g)

1/2 cup dark chocolate chips (85 g)

2 cups *grano cotto* (cooked wheat berries) (420 g)

Ground cinnamon

Mix ricotta, sugar, and vanilla extract in a medium bowl.

Cut candied fruit into small pieces.

Fold 1/4 cup chocolate chips and 1/2 cup candied fruit into the ricotta mixture.

Stir in grano cotto and a pinch of cinnamon. Mix well and pour into a large serving dish or individual dishes.

Decorate with remaining 1/4 cup chocolate chips and 1/2 cup candied fruit.

winter

INSALATA DI ARANCE E FINOCCHI

CECINA

IMPEPATA DI COZZE

MINESTRONE

PASTA ALLA CARBONARA

ORECCHIETTE ALLE CIME DI RAPA

SPAGHETTI ALLO SCOGLIO

TORTELLINI IN BRODO

RIBOLLITA

MINESTRA MARITATA

RISOTTO RADICCHIO E GORGONZOLA

CARCIOFI ALLA GIUDIA

CARCIOFI ALLA ROMANA

FARAONA RIPIENA DI CASTAGNE

COTECHINO CON LENTICCHIE

PORCHETTA

CALAMARI RIPIENI ALLA SICILIANA

OSSOBUCO

TRIGLIE AL FORNO

PANFORTE

BUCCELLATO

STRUFFOLI

ZABAIONE

CARTELLATE PUGLIESE

CROSTOLI

FRITTELLE DI RISO

TORTA MIMOSA

ZEPPOLE DI SAN GIUSEPPE

INSALATA DI ARANCE E FINOCCHI

ORANGE AND FENNEL SALAD WITH BLACK OLIVES

A fresh and light dish, *insalata di arance e finocchi* celebrates seasonal fruit and vegetables. The sweet and fragrant combination of orange and fennel is delicious as an antipasto or a side dish that pairs well with both fish and meat. While black olives are not always added, I believe the salty contrast complements the orange and fennel perfectly. If you can find them, I suggest using Taggiasche olives. Often, I'll combine them with oven-roasted black olives for an extra layer of flavor.

As for the quantities for this recipe, please feel free to improvise. I've provided an estimate for a salad that could serve two as a side dish or one as a healthy lunch.

SERVES 1 TO 2

1 large fennel bulb

2 medium oranges

1 cup black olives (150 g)

Extra-virgin olive oil

Salt

Freshly ground black pepper

Juice of 1 lemon (optional)

Clean fennel, removing green stalks and hard outer layer. Set aside fronds. Slice the bulb in half and remove the lower part of the core. Cut into 1/4-inch-thick slices with a sharp knife or mandolin.

Peel oranges and remove white pith. Cut into wedges or horizontal slices.

Arrange sliced fennel, oranges, and olives on a serving plate. Season to taste with extra-virgin olive oil, salt and pepper, and, if desired, a little lemon juice. Garnish with reserved feathery fennel fronds (also known as the beard).

CECINA

Though predominantly found in the northwest, *cecina* is a very popular street food throughout the Italian peninsula. Like many Italian foods, its name varies from region to region. On the Tuscan coast, it is called cecina, but you will also find it referred to as *torta di ceci*, *socca*, or *fainè*, depending on where you are.

With its characteristic crunchy, golden chickpea crust, cecina is one of the healthier street foods. During cold winter weekends when I lived in Tuscany, it was my favorite afternoon snack, bought hot from the local pizzeria. While many swear that it must be cooked in a pizza oven, I can assure you that you can recreate it at home. It is best eaten hot, as soon as it comes out of the oven, with a light sprinkling of salt and freshly cracked black pepper. Cecina is the perfect accompaniment to pre-dinner drinks.

SERVES 4

1 1/4 cups chickpea flour (150 g)

Salt

1/3 cup olive oil (75 ml), plus more for preparation

Freshly cracked black pepper, to serve

Mix chickpea flour and 1 teaspoon salt in a large bowl. Make a well in the middle and pour in 2 cups room temperature water. Whisk until there are no visible lumps. Add olive oil and whisk again. Cover the bowl with plastic wrap and let rest 3 to 4 hours.

Preheat oven to the maximum temperature (as hot as it will go!) as cecina is traditionally cooked in a wood-fired pizza oven.

Brush a 12-inch (30-cm) round pizza tray with olive oil. Whisk the mixture again before pouring it on the tray. Using a pastry brush, flick some olive oil onto the dough.

Bake in preheated oven 25 minutes, or until the top is golden brown and crackled. Season to taste with salt and freshly cracked black pepper, slice, and serve hot.

IMPEPATA DI COZZE

PEPPERED MUSSELS

Seafood in all forms is a staple during winter festivities in Italy, and mussels are always a perfect choice for any antipasto. This recipe is versatile and can be served either as an appetizer or a main course. It is light, inexpensive, and very easy to make. Simplicity is key, as this recipe uses only a few ingredients to let the natural flavors of the mussels shine.

SERVES 4

4 1/2 pounds mussels (2 kg)

2 cloves garlic, peeled and sliced

1/2 cup white wine (120 ml)

3 tablespoons olive oil

Freshly cracked black pepper

4 to 5 tablespoons fresh flat-leaf parsley, chopped, to serve

Make sure all the mussels are closed; discard any that are open, cracked, or broken. Clean by removing and discarding the beards and scraping off any impurities on the shells with steel wool. Soak in a bowl of cold water and rinse thoroughly under cold running water.

Place drained mussels in a large saucepan. Add garlic, wine, olive oil, and a generous amount of pepper. Cover and cook over high heat 4 to 5 minutes.

Discard any unopened mussels, and using a slotted spoon, transfer the rest to a second saucepan. Filter cooking liquid from the first pan through a fine sieve and return to the second pan with the cooked mussels.

Add more freshly cracked black pepper. Simmer another 2 to 3 minutes, or until it comes to a boil. Sprinkle with chopped parsley and serve immediately.

Fresh mussels—and even cooked ones—should smell like the ocean, with a briny, salty smell. If they have a strong, fishy, or foul odor, they are bad and should not be eaten.

It is always preferable to grind pepper at the moment you need it, as this ensures a more aromatic and intense flavor. For this recipe, I use a mortar and pestle.

MINESTRONE

SERVES MANY!

3 ribs celery

2 carrots, peeled

2 small onions

1/2 cup olive oil (120 ml)

2 quarts vegetable broth (2 L) (see recipe on page 210)

1 1/2 cups chopped diced pumpkin and/or sweet potato (300 g)

1 (14-ounce) can crushed tomatoes (400 g)

2 bay leaves

Parmigiano Reggiano cheese rind

Fresh basil

1 handful savoy cabbage

1 handful kale

1 handful chard

1 (15-ounce) can borlotti beans (425 g), drained

1 (15-ounce) can kidney beans (425 g), drained

Salt

Freshly cracked black pepper, chopped flat-leaf parsley, and grated Parmigiano Reggiano, to serve

Small pasta (optional)

Cut celery and carrots into 1/2-inch pieces. Finely chop 2 onions. Heat olive oil in a large saucepan and add celery, carrots, and onions. Cook about 10 minutes, or until onions are translucent.

Add broth, pumpkin, tomatoes, bay leaves, Parmigiano Reggiano rind, and basil and bring to a boil. Stir in leafy vegetables and canned beans. Reduce heat and keep at a rolling simmer about 30 minutes. Remove bay leaves and cheese rind and season to taste with salt and pepper.

To serve, sprinkle with parsley, a generous amount of Parmigiano Reggiano, and freshly cracked black pepper.

If adding pasta such as pastina or ditalini, bring a large pot of salted water to a boil and cook according to package directions. Drain and add portions of pasta to soup bowls. Then ladle the minestrone on top.

There is no right or wrong way to make minestrone and it is undoubtedly one of the best comfort foods for a cold winter's day.

The base always includes a *soffritto* (sauté) of celery, carrots and onions, and then, like a blank canvas, the other ingredients are added. Minestrone is a fantastic way to use up vegetables that are a little past their prime but still perfectly fine to eat. Leafy vegetables such as spinach, chard, Savoy cabbage and kale are ideal, as are zucchini, cauliflower, Romanesco, potatoes and pumpkin. I also like to add tomatoes or a couple of cups of tomato sauce. Minestrone can be completely vegetarian, or you can add guanciale or pancetta.

Minestrone needs to cook for 35 to 40 minutes for the vegetables to soften and release their flavors. If using dried beans, it is best to soak them overnight; the cooking time may then need to be extended up to one to two hours. Alternatively, you can use canned beans, which are convenient and still delicious. Borlotti, cannellini and kidney beans are all popular choices. Chickpeas can also be added. If you do not have vegetable broth on hand, you can substitute it with water and a couple of bouillon cubes.

PASTA ALLA CARBONARA

A traditional Roman dish, pasta alla carbonara is one of Italy's most celebrated. The only ingredients are Pecorino Romano cheese, eggs, guanciale, black pepper, and pasta. Variations should never be accepted—if you add garlic, leeks, peas, mushrooms, parsley, or (God forbid) cream, please use a different name for this pasta dish!

The origins of carbonara are unclear. Some believe it was brought to Lazio from Umbria by coal men (*carbonari*), which would explain the name. Interestingly, the earliest known recipe dates back to the 1950s, where it is described as a dish prepared for American soldiers whose meal rations included bacon and eggs. Others suggest that homesick British troops longing for a traditional breakfast inspired Italians to adapt these ingredients into a pasta dish.

Using the best ingredients will elevate your pasta alla carbonara to a whole new level. The Italian word for cheek is *guancia*, which is why cured pork jowl or cheek is called *guanciale*. If you can't find it, you can substitute pancetta or bacon. Please use the freshest free-range eggs and a good-quality black pepper, ground just before cooking. I can't finish without mentioning the pasta: High-quality pasta extruded through a bronze die creates a rough, porous surface that allows the delicious sauce to cling to it.

Making pasta alla carbonara isn't difficult and once you've mastered it, you should be left wanting to lick the bowl and break out singing "That's Amore!"

SERVES 2

7 ounces guanciale (200 g)

4 eggs (2 whole eggs and 2 yolks)

2 1/2 cups finely grated Pecorino Romano (250 g), plus more to serve

Freshly cracked black pepper

1/2 pound rigatoni (225 g)

Bring a large pot of salted water to a boil.

Using a sharp knife, trim guanciale, removing thick skin and any tough, dried sections on the side covered with spices. Cut into cubes. Place in a large pan over low heat until crisp and golden. Turn off the heat and set aside.

Beat egg and yolks in a medium bowl, adding Pecorino Romano a little at a time, until you have a thick paste. You might not use all the cheese, or you might require more; it depends on the size of the eggs. Add a generous dose of freshly cracked black pepper.

Place rigatoni in boiling water and cook 2 minutes less than the packet instructions until al dente. Drain pasta and return to the same pot. Stir in most of the guanciale with the pan drippings, reserving a little guanciale for garnish.

While keeping the pan off the heat to prevent an unsightly scrambled egg pasta, add the egg and cheese mixture, stirring vigorously. The heat from the pasta will cook the egg and cheese and create a luxurious, creamy sauce.

To serve, sprinkle with freshly grated Pecorino Romano, reserved guanciale, and freshly cracked black pepper.

ORECCHIETTE ALLE CIME DI RAPA

ORECCHIETTE WITH TURNIP GREENS

Homemade orecchiette from durum wheat semolina cooked with turnip greens is one of the most typical peasant dishes of Puglia, particularly in the province of Bari. The secret lies in cooking the orecchiette in the same water used for cooking the turnip greens (or sometimes, broccoli rabe) as the pasta absorbs the aromas and flavors of the vegetable.

SERVES 4

Extra-virgin olive oil

3/4 cup dry breadcrumbs (90 g)

1 bunch turnip greens or broccoli rabe

Salt

1 clove garlic, peeled and finely chopped

3 to 4 anchovies

1 pound orecchiette (455 g)

1 fresh chili pepper, finely chopped

Heat a generous splash of olive oil in a large, deep pan. Add breadcrumbs and toast 2 to 3 minutes, stirring often until evenly browned. Remove and set aside.

Remove stems and any fibrous parts from turnip greens. Keep only the tops and the most tender leaves. Discard any that are yellow or unappealing. Rinse well under plenty of cold running water.

Bring a large pot of water to a boil. Add turnip greens and a pinch of salt. Reduce heat and simmer 5 to 10 minutes, or until tender. Remove leaves with a slotted spoon and set aside. Leave cooking water in the pan and set aside. You will use this water to cook the pasta.

Place garlic, anchovies, and a splash of olive oil in the same pan you used to toast the breadcrumbs. Stir over medium heat until anchovies have dissolved.

Return the reserved water used to cook the turnip greens to a boil. Add orecchiette and cook 1 to 2 minutes less than package directions until very al dente, remembering to reserve the cooking water.

Add reserved cooked greens to the pan with garlic and anchovies. Stir continually over high heat 1 to 2 minutes. Add 1 to 2 ladles pasta water. Drain orecchiette, reserving the water. Transfer pasta to the pan with the greens, adding reserved pasta water if needed. Stir, continuing to cook 1 to 2 minutes, or until orecchiette is ready.

Sprinkle with reserved breadcrumbs and chopped chili pepper to serve.

Though cheese isn't usually added to this dish, a grated Parmigiano Reggiano, Pecorino Romano, or even a hard, salted ricotta would be a nice addition—as would a little drizzle of extra-virgin olive oil.

SPAGHETTI ALLO SCOGLIO

SEAFOOD SPAGHETTI

Traditional to Southern Italy, specifically Campania, this first course is known as *spaghetti allo scoglio. Scoglio* translates to "rock," which is apt since most of the ingredients are found near rocky coastlines.

SERVES 4

1 pound clams and mussels (455 g)

1 (1/2 pound) baby squid (225 g)

Sea salt

Extra-virgin olive oil

8 prawns or scampi

2 cloves garlic, peeled and grated

2 cups fresh flat-leaf parsley, chopped

1/2 cup white wine (120 ml)

1 cup cherry tomatoes (150 g) or 1/2 cup tomato sauce (120 ml)

1 pound spaghetti or linguine (455 g)

Inspect clams and mussels and discard any that are broken or open. Purge clams of sand by placing them in a bowl of cold salted water 1 to 2 hours. Clean mussels by removing and discarding the beards and scraping off any impurities on the shells with steel wool. Soak in a bowl of cold water and rinse thoroughly under cold running water.

Cut the tentacles from the squid and slice the body into rings. Set aside.

Transfer clams and mussels to a large saucepan. Cover and cook over medium-high heat 4 to 5 minutes. Remove from heat as soon as shells open to avoid overcooking the delicate meat.

Remove clams and mussels with a slotted spoon and set aside. Strain their cooking water through a fine-meshed sieve or clean kitchen towel to ensure no grains of sand remain. Set strained water aside. Shuck half the clams and mussels, leaving half intact.

Bring a large pot of salted water to a boil.

Heat 2 tablespoons olive oil in a separate very large, deep pan. Add prawns. Cover and simmer 5 minutes. When prawns have cooled, shell and set aside.

In the same pan, add 2 tablespoons olive oil. Sauté garlic over medium heat 1 minute. Add squid and 1/4 cup parsley. Cook, covered, 5 minutes. Uncover and increase heat to high. Add wine and tomatoes and cook 2 minutes.

Return peeled prawns to the pan and cook 1 minute. Add shucked and shelled clams and mussels, 1/4 cup parsley, and the filtered cooking water. Cover and cook over very low heat no longer than 10 minutes.

Using a slotted spoon, remove the seafood from the pan and set aside. Leave the liquid in the pan.

Add spaghetti to boiling water and cook for half the time on the package directions. Drain and transfer to the pan with the seafood liquids. Simmer over medium heat to finish cooking the spaghetti. Season to taste with sea salt if necessary. Add a generous splash of olive oil, remaining parsley, and all the seafood and stir well over high heat 1 minute. Serve immediately.

TORTELLINI IN BRODO

A true glory of Italian cuisine, *tortellini in brodo* is a beloved staple in Emilia-Romagna, where it is an essential dish on most Christmas Day tables. This recipe often varies depending on family traditions and is typically handed down through generations. While the ingredients don't change much—the filling always including pork meat, mortadella, prosciutto crudo, and Parmigiano Reggiano—the proportions are a closely guarded secret within each family.

SERVES 4

1 tablespoon unsalted butter

2 to 3 fresh sage leaves

1 bay leaf

1 sprig fresh rosemary

4 ounces pork loin, sliced (115 g)

Salt and pepper

4 ounces mortadella (115 g)

4 ounces prosciutto (115 g)

1 cup freshly grated Parmigiano Reggiano (100 g), plus more to serve

1 egg

Nutmeg, freshly grated

Fresh egg pasta (see recipe on page 219)

Flour for rolling out pasta

2 quarts broth (2 L) (see recipe on page 211)

To make the filling, melt butter in a pan over medium heat. Add sage leaves, bay leaf, and rosemary. Add sliced pork. Brown and cook evenly on both sides. Season to taste with salt and pepper.

Place cooked pork and 1 tablespoon pan drippings in a food processor or blender and pulse roughly. Add mortadella and prosciutto and pulse again. Transfer to a medium bowl. Stir in 1 cup Parmigiano Reggiano, egg, and nutmeg to taste until the mixture is smooth. (Traditionally, the tortellini filling would be processed through a meat grinder, similar to the method used for making sausage.) Refrigerate until ready to use.

Lightly dust work surface with flour and roll out pasta following instructions on page 216. With the help of a ruler, cut pasta into 1 1/2-inch squares. Cover cut pasta with plastic wrap to prevent it from drying out until you are ready to assemble the tortellini.

Place 1/4 teaspoon filling in the center of each square of pasta. Fold corner to corner to form a triangle. Press firmly along the seams to secure and squeeze out any air pockets, then overlap the two corners at the base and press to seal. If the pasta becomes slightly dry, you can use a small amount of water to help secure the seams.

Bring broth to a gentle boil and cook tortellini for a couple of minutes until they rise to the surface. Taste one to ensure the pasta is cooked. Serve tortellini in broth. Top with freshly grated Parmigiano Reggiano.

Making tortellini is undoubtedly time-consuming and a labor of love, but they can be frozen and cooked directly from the freezer. This means you can plan ahead, making this one of the easier dishes to get on the table during the hectic moments that characterize everyone's kitchens on Christmas Day. Of course, you can also buy good-quality tortellini and cook them in your homemade broth.

RIBOLLITA

TUSCAN BREAD, BEAN, AND VEGETABLE SOUP

SERVES 8

1 pound dried cannellini beans (455 g) or 1 (15-ounce) can (425 g), drained

Salt

1 clove garlic, peeled

1 sprig fresh rosemary

Extra-virgin olive oil

1 bunch kale

1 head savoy cabbage

1 bunch Swiss chard

4 ribs celery with leaves, chopped

2 carrots, chopped

1 onion, chopped

1 large potato, peeled and diced

1 cup canned crushed tomatoes (240 ml) or 2 large tomatoes, finely chopped

5 sprigs fresh thyme (leaves only)

2 cups stale whole-wheat Tuscan bread (200 g), crust on, cut into large cubes

Freshly ground black pepper, to serve

If using dried cannellini beans, soak in 6 cups water and 1/2 tablespoon salt a minimum of 8 hours or overnight.

Transfer beans and soaking water to a large pot. Add garlic, rosemary, and a generous splash of olive oil. Boil gently 1 hour, or until beans are cooked and soft, adding extra water if needed.

Remove 1/2 cup beans and set aside.

Purée remaining beans in the pot with an immersion blender. (Or transfer to a food processor or blender, purée, and set aside.)

Wash kale, cabbage, and Swiss chard. Drain, chop roughly into 1 1/2-inch pieces, and set aside.

In a large saucepan, sauté celery, carrots, and onion in 1/3 cup olive oil over medium-high heat until onion is translucent and slightly golden. Add puréed beans, chopped leafy greens, potato, tomatoes, thyme, and 4 cups water. Cover and cook over low heat about 1 hour.

Stir in 1/2 cup reserved whole beans and bread cubes. Cook 5 to 10 minutes.

Let sit a minimum of 4 hours, or preferably overnight, to give bread ample time to absorb the soup.

When ready to eat, reheat and add a little freshly cracked black pepper and a drizzle of olive oil. Serve with fresh, rustic Tuscan bread on the side.

A staple of *cucina povera*, *ribollita* was born out of necessity, using leftover minestrone or vegetable soup thickened with stale bread. The name means "reboiled," as it was traditionally made in large batches and reheated over several days, with flavors deepening each time. Packed with *cavolo nero* (Tuscan black kale), cannellini beans, and rustic bread, ribollita is a humble yet deeply satisfying dish that embodies the Tuscan philosophy of wasting nothing while making something delicious.

MINESTRA MARITATA

WEDDING SOUP

SERVES 10 TO 12

1 whole chicken

2 pounds chuck roast (900 g)

Olive oil

3 ribs celery, finely chopped

2 white onions, finely chopped

2 carrots, finely chopped

6 to 8 pork ribs

1 (24-ounce) Neapolitan salami (680 g)

1 cup chopped pancetta (150 g)

2 bay leaves

1 teaspoon black peppercorns

Salt

1 head smooth escarole

1 head curly endive

1 savoy cabbage

1 cabbage

1 bunch chicory

1 bunch Swiss chard

1 bunch borage

Parmigiano Reggiano and freshly cracked black pepper, to serve

Cut hen in half. Rinse under cold water and pat dry. Cut chuck roast into 1-inch pieces.

Heat a generous splash of olive oil in a large, deep pan. Add celery, onions and carrots and saute until onions are translucent.

Add chicken, beef, pork ribs, whole salami and pancetta and cover with about 2 gallons cold water. Add bay leaves, peppercorns and 1 tablespoon salt. Bring to a boil. Reduce heat and simmer at least 3 hours, occasionally skimming off any fat or impurities that rise to the surface.

Bring a pot of salted water to a boil and prepare a large bowl of ice water.

Wash and roughly chop leafy greens. Blanch each type separately in boiling water, adjusting the cooking time for each—approximately 2 to 3 minutes, or until tender. Using a slotted spoon, transfer blanched greens to ice bath, and set aside.

When the broth is ready, filter it through a fine-mesh strainer into another large pot. Remove all the meat. Take the meat off the hen and pork ribs and cut salami into slices and add to the pot with the filtered broth. Strain blanched greens. Add to pot and bring to a boil.

Serve piping hot, garnished with shavings of Parmigiano Reggiano and freshly cracked black pepper.

Minestra maritata is traditionally served during Christmas and Easter meals. *Maritata* means "married," a nod to the marriage of flavors between the meats and leafy green vegetables. Contrary to common belief overseas, Italian wedding soup has nothing to do with celebrating a marriage between two people nor is it typically part of a wedding meal. This is a highly adaptable recipe that varies from family to family and depends on the availability of vegetables at any given time of the year. It is time-consuming, so I suggest spreading the preparation over two days: start with the meat broth on the first day, and cook the vegetables on the second day.

RISOTTO RADICCHIO E GORGONZOLA

Risotto with radicchio (red chicory) is a dish traditional to Veneto, specifically Treviso, where the local Radicchio di Treviso has been granted Protected Geographical Indication (PGI) status by the European Union. This designation ensures that the radicchio is grown, processed, and packaged in a specific area of Veneto. This variety of chicory is dark red with white streaks, has a bitter taste, and is quite crunchy. Although it is most popular in risotto, it is also used in salads.

Traditionally, cooks opt for creamy, sweet gorgonzola, but it ultimately comes down to personal taste. If, like me, you prefer your gorgonzola spicier and drier, choose one that is more pungent. I always buy a little extra—it's nice to nibble on while you are stirring the risotto. And of course, be generous when you sprinkle the gorgonzola on top of the risotto before serving.

SERVES 4

1 quart broth (see page 211) (1 L)

2 to 3 tablespoons extra virgin olive oil

2 tablespoons unsalted butter (30 g)

4 cups radicchio, cut into strips (200 g), divided

1 onion, finely chopped

1 cup uncooked Arborio or Carnaroli rice (200 g)

1/2 cup white wine (120 ml)

4 ounces gorgonzola (100 g), more to serve

1/2 cup cream (120 ml)

Freshly grated Parmigiano Reggiano

Bring broth to a boil, then reduce heat to maintain a hot temperature.

Heat oil and butter in a saucepan. Add 2 cups radicchio and chopped onion. Saute until onion starts to brown. Add rice and toast about 1 minute, stirring continually. Add wine and continue to stir until wine has evaporated.

Add hot broth to the rice, one ladle at a time, stirring gently and continually until the broth is absorbed. When you have added half the broth, add remaining radicchio. Continue adding 1 ladle of broth at a time and stirring until rice is cooked.

Remove rind from gorgonzola. Cut cheese into small pieces and place in a pan with cream over low heat. Stir occasionally until gorgonzola has completely melted.

Remove risotto from heat and stir in cheese sauce and Parmigiano Reggiano. Cover and let rest a few minutes. Serve hot and crumble a little extra gorgonzola on top of each bowl; it will gradually melt as you enjoy the risotto.

CARCIOFI ALLA GIUDIA

JEWISH-STYLE ARTICHOKES

These twice-fried artichokes are thought to have originated in Rome's Jewish ghetto in the sixteenth century. If you happen to be in Rome when the local artichokes are in season—from late October to March—you absolutely have to try this dish. Although I usually enjoy these as street food or when dining out, they can certainly be made at home. Any type of artichoke can be used, but in Italy, we prefer *mammole* for their tenderness and thornless nature.

Jewish-style artichokes are fried twice. The first frying at a lower temperature cooks the artichoke uniformly, while the second frying in a much hotter oil turns the leaves golden and crisp—so crunchy it's like eating artichoke chips.

SERVES 4

4 artichokes, cleaned

Juice of 1 lemon

Salt

Freshly cracked black pepper

2 quarts olive oil (2 L)

White wine (optional)

Remove and discard the outermost leaves from artichokes. Soak artichokes in a bowl of cold water and lemon juice about 10 minutes.

Drain and pat dry. Holding the stems, press the artichokes down on a work surface so the leaves separate and open up. You can also use your hands to gently pry them open. Season inside and out with salt and pepper.

Heat olive oil to 265°F (130°C) in a large, deep saucepan. Place artichokes in oil head-side down and, turning occasionally, cook 10 to 15 minutes, or until soft in the middle. Remove from oil, drain on paper towels, and let cool.

Reheat oil until boiling hot. Spray artichokes with water or, if desired, white wine. One at a time, fry submerged artichokes, head-side down, about 5 minutes. As they fry, push down so the leaves open like the petals of a flower.

Remove artichokes, drain on paper towels, sprinkle with salt, and serve immediately.

Rubbing a cut lemon on your hands before you clean artichokes keeps them from getting stained.

CARCIOFI ALLA ROMANA

ROMAN-STYLE ARTICHOKES

If you visit any Roman market during artichoke season, you will see storekeepers spending their entire mornings peeling and cleaning artichokes. Artichokes should be cleaned without mercy, so we sometimes have to do even more when we get home which is better that than serving a fibrous artichoke.

And when in Rome . . . one must try *carciofi alla romana*. It is important to note that the whole artichoke is edible when it arrives on your plate.

SERVES 4

4 artichokes, cleaned

Juice of 1 lemon

1 small bunch fresh Roman mint

1 cup fresh flat-leaf parsley

1 clove garlic, peeled

Extra-virgin olive oil

Salt

Freshly cracked black pepper

Tear off the artichokes' outer leaves with your hands. Cut the end off each stem and slice the tips off the heads. If your variety has an internal beard or choke, remove it. Peel the stem and tidy the base of the artichoke with a sharp paring knife. Soak artichokes in a bowl of cold water and lemon juice. Cover with paper towels and set aside.

Blend Roman mint, parsley, garlic, and olive oil in a food processor or blender. Mix in a pinch of salt and freshly cracked black pepper.

Drain artichokes and pat lightly with paper towels to remove excess water. Press the herbal mixture in between the artichoke leaves and rub over the heads.

Place artichokes head-side down in a saucepan, keeping them close together so they don't spread open. Add remaining herbal mixture to the pan. Add 1/4 cup olive oil and 1 inch of water. Wet a piece of unbleached parchment paper under running water. Squeeze until damp and place over artichokes.

Cover with a lid and place pan over medium-low heat. When water starts to boil, reduce heat to low. After 30 minutes test artichokes with a fork to see if they are soft. If not, continue cooking until they are tender, making sure water doesn't evaporate completely as you risk burning artichokes and the base of the saucepan.

Enjoy eating these with a squeeze of fresh lemon juice and a little cracked black pepper.

Roman mint or calamint—*nepitella* in Italian—is a cross between oregano and mint.

FARAONA RIPIENA DI CASTAGNE

GUINEA FOWL WITH CHESTNUT STUFFING

SERVES 6

12 ounces chestnuts (340 g), roasted

1/4 cup (1/2 stick) unsalted butter (60 g)

4 tablespoons olive oil

3 ribs celery, finely chopped

1 medium onion, finely chopped

1 small carrot, finely chopped

1 bunch fresh flat-leaf parsley, chopped

1 bunch fresh thyme

2/3 cup pistachios (110 g)

1/2 pound ground veal (225 g)

1/2 pound ground pork (225 g)

2 slices Tuscan bread, finely chopped

1/2 cup mixture currants and candied peel (80 g)

1 cup chicken broth (240 ml)

1 (3- to 4-pound) guinea fowl (1.4 to 1.8 kg), deboned

3 to 4 slices speck or bacon

Sprigs fresh rosemary

Salt and pepper

Peel and roughly chop roasted chestnuts. Let butter come to room temperature.

Preheat oven to 350°F (180°C).

To make the stuffing, heat olive oil in a large pan over medium heat, and sauté celery, onion, and carrot until onion is translucent. Let cool.

Stir in handful of parsley, 1 1/2 tablespoons thyme leaves, chopped chestnuts, pistachios, ground meats, bread, and the mixture of currants and candied peel.

Add broth and mix everything thoroughly with your hands so the bread absorbs the broth.

Place bird skin-side down on your work surface. Arrange stuffing down the middle in a loaf-like shape, ensuring it is evenly distributed. Fold the bird around the stuffing and lay the speck slices along the seam. Tie the bird together with butcher's twine, inserting 2 long sprigs rosemary next to the speck. Tie the wings close to the body.

Mix remaining 1 1/2 tablespoons thyme leaves with butter and rub all over the bird. Season with salt and pepper and place on a roasting rack, speck side up.

Roast at 350°F (180°C) for 1 1/2 hours, or until a meat thermometer inserted in the thickest part of the breast reads 165°F (74°C). Let rest at least 20 minutes before serving.

I recommend cooking the chestnuts the night before. Cut a cross or an X into the hard outer skin of each one with a sharp knife. To roast, place on a baking tray at 400°F (200°C) for 20 minutes or until they are soft. This will bring out their sweetness, but you can also boil them in a saucepan of water for 20 minutes or until they are soft. I actually like to boil them for about 15 minutes and then roast them in the oven for another 10 to 15 minutes until they split open a little.

COTECHINO CON LENTICCHIE

RICH, SPICED PORK SAUSAGE WITH LENTILS

New Year's Eve in Italy is marked by a large, festive meal known as *cenone di* San Silvestro (Saint Sylvester's big dinner) or cenone di Capodanno (New Year's Eve big dinner), where you would be hard-pressed to find a family get-together or dinner party that doesn't include *cotechino con lenticchie*. The tradition of eating lentils to celebrate the New Year dates back to ancient Roman times, when a pouch of lentils was given as a gift with the hope that they would turn into gold coins, symbolizing prosperity and good fortune for the year ahead. Even today it is considered a good omen if you start the new year eating lentils—the more you eat, the richer you will be, apparently!

Historically, this is a recipe that anyone could afford, even poor peasant families. Cotechino is a richly seasoned pork sausage from Emilia-Romagna. While it can be purchased uncooked from a specialty butcher, most people buy it precooked in a vacuum-packed pouch, which definitely speeds up the preparation of this meal. All you have to do is prepare the lentils and heat up the cotechino.

SERVES 4

2 cups dried lentils (400 g)

5 shallots, peeled and finely chopped

3 to 4 ribs celery, finely chopped

2 small carrots, finely chopped

Olive oil

1/3 cup pancetta (80 g)

2 bay leaves

1/2 cup white wine (120 ml)

1 cup canned crushed tomatoes (240 ml)

1 quart broth of choice (1 L) (see recipes on pages 210–211)

1 store-bought cotechino or zampone (precooked)

Salt and pepper

Preheat oven to 350°F (180°C).

Rinse lentils in a sieve under cold running water. Let soak 2 hours in cold water (check cooking instructions for the lentils you buy because some don't need to be pre-soaked).

Place shallots, celery, and carrots in a Dutch oven or deep, oven-safe pan with 1 to 2 generous splashes of olive oil. Sauté slowly over medium heat until shallots are slightly brown.

Add pancetta and bay leaves and stir frequently about 5 minutes. Stir in wine and simmer 5 minutes until it has reduced. Add drained lentils and tomatoes with juice, mixing well. Pour in broth, adding water if necessary to ensure lentils are completely covered.

Continue to simmer about 1 hour, or until lentils are soft, stirring frequently so they don't stick to the bottom of the pan. Season sparingly with salt and pepper. Top up with extra broth (or water) if lentils seem dry and undercooked. Discard bay leaves once lentils have finished cooking.

Prepare the cotechino according to package directions, which typically recommend boiling the vacuum-packed sausage in water 30 minutes. Drain juice from the packet and slice the sausage. You can serve the cotechino atop the lentils immediately, but some people like to quickly sear the sliced sausage in a frying pan first.

PORCHETTA

Porchetta originated in the central Italian town of Ariccia which holds a weekend-long festival every September to celebrate this savory delight.

Though it makes for a delicious main course—like roast pork—you will find porchetta is a common street food throughout Italy, sliced thinly in a panino or as a topping on pizza *bianca*.

Known for its crispy skin and tender meat, porchetta is usually seasoned with sage, rosemary, fennel seeds, salt, and black pepper. If adding garlic, do so sparingly so it doesn't overpower the other herbs.

SERVES 4 TO 6

8 to 12 fresh sage leaves

8 sprigs fresh rosemary

1/4 cup fresh thyme leaves

2 tablespoons salt

2 tablespoons fennel seeds

2 cloves garlic, peeled (optional)

1 teaspoon black peppercorns

1/4 cup olive oil (60 ml)

1 (8-pound) pork belly (3.6 kg), boneless, skin on

2 (1/2-pound) pork tenderloins (455 g)

1 cup dry white wine (240 ml)

To make the seasoning, place sage, 5 sprigs rosemary, thyme, salt, 1 tablespoon fennel seeds, garlic, and peppercorns in a food processor and pulse to combine. Stir in olive oil and set aside.

Using a very sharp knife, score the pork belly skin in lines, being careful not to cut into the meat. (Or you can ask your butcher to do this.)

Lay pork belly skin-side down. Sprinkle generously with the herbal seasoning and rub into the meat.

Place pork tenderloins on top of the pork belly and roll the pork belly around it. Tie with butcher's twine in multiple places, as tightly as possible, equally spaced.

Wrap meat in a kitchen towel and place in refrigerator a minimum of 6 hours, or preferably overnight.

Preheat oven to 425°F (220°C).

Add wine, 1 cup water, remaining 3 sprigs rosemary, and remaining fennel seeds to a roasting pan. Unwrap porchetta and rewrap in aluminum foil and place on a roasting rack set inside the roasting pan. Roast at 425°F (220 degrees C) for 1 hour.

Remove the foil and reduce the temperature to 400°F (200°C). Roast for 3 1/2 to 4 hours, uncovered, turning the porchetta every 30 minutes so the skin cooks and crackles evenly around.

Let rest for at least 20 to 30 minutes before slicing to retain juices.

Calculate 1 hour of cooking time for every 2 pounds of meat. If you cook a smaller version, you don't need to wrap in foil as it will only be in the oven 1 to 1 1/2 hours. Porchetta should reach an internal temperature of 167 to 176°F (75 to 80°C).

CALAMARI RIPIENI ALLA SICILIANA

STUFFED CALAMARI

Stuffed calamari are delicious, with numerous variations not only in fillings, but also in cooking techniques—whether baked in the oven or grilled. The saltiness from the capers and anchovies complements the Marsala-soaked currants, imparting distinct Sicilian flavors.

SERVES 4

1/3 cup currants or sultanas (50 g)

1/3 cup Marsala (80 ml)

1 cup cherry tomatoes (150 g)

4 fresh squid

Extra-virgin olive oil

4 anchovy filets in oil (undrained)

2 1/2 cups breadcrumbs (375 g), plus more for serving

1/3 cup pistachios (45 g), roughly chopped, plus more for serving

1 bunch fresh flat-leaf parsley, chopped

1/4 cup capers (35 g)

1/4 cup chopped olives (50 g)

Zest of 1 lemon

1 1/4 cups freshly grated pecorino Romano (125 g)

Salt

Freshly cracked black pepper

Place currants in a small bowl, cover with Marsala, and set aside.

Roughly chop 8 cherry tomatoes and set aside.

Preheat oven to 325°F (160°C).

Cut the tentacles off the squid and chop them into small pieces, leaving the mantles intact.

Heat 2 tablespoons olive oil in a pan and add anchovy filets and chopped tentacles. Sauté 2 to 3 minutes, or until anchovies are completely dissolved.

Mix breadcrumbs, 1/3 cup pistachios, and parsley in a bowl.

In a second pan, heat 2 tablespoons olive oil over medium-low heat and carefully toast breadcrumb mixture 2 to 3 minutes, stirring continually to ensure it doesn't burn.

Drain currants. Stir currants, 8 reserved chopped tomatoes, capers, olives, lemon zest, Pecorino Romano, and pan-fried anchovies and tentacles into breadcrumb mixture. If it seems too dry, add a little olive oil.

Using a spoon, delicately fill squid mantles about three-quarters full with stuffing. Since squid tend to shrink during cooking, avoid overfilling to prevent them from breaking open. Secure ends of the squid with a toothpick.

Place stuffed squid in a baking dish with remaining whole cherry tomatoes. Drizzle with olive oil and sprinkle with fresh breadcrumbs and pistachios.

Bake at 325°F (160°C) for 30 minutes and serve hot with roasted cherry tomatoes.

OSSOBUCO

Some recipes for *ossobuco* call for tomatoes, but in Milan, where it originated, they don't, and neither do I. *Ossobuco* translates to "bone with a hole," which describes the cross-cut veal shanks that make this dish so remarkable. It is important to buy your ossobuco from a good butcher, and maybe spend a little more for top-quality meat. It will be worth it and always much better than having the disappointment of preparing and cooking something for hours and discovering the meat isn't tender. When cooked properly, the meat falls off the bone.

SERVES 4

1 cup all-purpose flour (120 g)

Salt and pepper

8 veal shanks, cut at least 1-inch thick

Olive oil

1/4 cup (1/2 stick) unsalted butter (60 g)

3 ribs celery, finely chopped

2 large carrots, finely chopped

1 large red onion, finely chopped

2 cloves garlic, peeled (optional)

1 cup white wine (240 ml)

1 cup broth of choice (240 ml) (see recipes on page 210–211)

8 sprigs fresh thyme

Zest of 1 lemon, to serve

1 bunch fresh flat-leaf parsley, chopped, to serve

Preheat oven to 325°F (160°C).

Place flour in a wide, shallow bowl or large plate and stir in 1 teaspoon salt and 1 teaspoon pepper.

Snip the membrane that surrounds each piece of veal in 3 or 4 places to prevent the meat from curling while it cooks.

Coat each veal shank on both sides in the seasoned flour, shake off the excess, and set aside.

Heat olive oil and butter in a large pan, until butter melts and starts to sizzle. Working in batches, sauté veal on each side until golden and place in a large baking dish.

In the same pan, add a splash of olive oil. Add celery, carrots, and onion, and sauté until onion softens. If adding garlic, do so now. Add wine and broth and bring to a boil. Pour over veal in the baking dish. Sprinkle with thyme, salt, and pepper. Cover with aluminum foil and bake at 325°F (160°C) for 2 1/2 hours.

Garnish with lemon zest and parsley and serve.

A great comfort-food dish, ossobuco is traditionally served with *risotto alla milanese* (see recipe on page 110), but it also pairs well with creamy mashed potatoes, soft polenta, or even couscous.

TRIGLIE AL FORNO

ROASTED RED MULLET

During the festive season in Italy, particularly on Christmas Eve and New Year's Eve, seafood plays a significant part of the celebration.

Historically, Romans held red mullets in high regard, even raising them as pets and training them to respond when called. Some of these fish were so valued that they could fetch their weight in silver. Nowadays, red mullets are much more affordable, and their striking salmon-pink color makes them an attractive addition to any table. This recipe is quick and easy, making it an excellent second course for large family meals during the holidays.

If the red mullets are large, one per person will suffice. Typically, they are medium size, and you would need two per serving.

SERVES 4

8 medium triglie (red mullets)

2 lemons

Olive oil

Fresh thyme leaves

2 cloves garlic, peeled and minced

Coarse salt

4 to 8 potatoes (optional)

Preheat oven to 400°F (200°C).

If your fishmonger hasn't cleaned the fish for you, do it yourself by rinsing under cold running water, making an incision on the belly with a sharp knife, and removing all the entrails. Scrape the scales off from tail to head and rinse again. I prefer to cook the fish whole, but you may want to remove the head and fins.

Cut 1 lemon into thin slices and finely grate the peel of the other.

Line a baking dish with parchment paper and grease with olive oil.

Insert half a lemon slice and some thyme leaves and garlic into the belly of each fish.

Brush fish with olive oil and sprinkle with finely grated lemon peel and coarse salt according to your preference.

Bake at 400°F (200°C) for 15 to 20 minutes.

I like to serve this with roasted potatoes. Slice 4 to 8 potatoes Hasselback-style. Drizzle with olive oil and salt to taste. Put them in the oven first, and add the fish 30 to 45 minutes later so both are ready at the same time.

PANFORTE

A classic Italian Christmas dessert, *panforte* ("strong bread") is a dense, rich, and aptly named confection. This versatile recipe allows you to use any combination of nuts and fruits, making it perfect for incorporating leftovers from other holiday baking.

Panforte keeps exceptionally well, offering a delicious treat that can be enjoyed after the holiday season is over, possibly even into the new year—though it's so delightful, it might be gone much sooner.

The tradition of gifting panforte dates back to medieval times, when it was often presented as a symbolic offering to monasteries and churches, prized for its luxurious ingredients like nuts, honey, and spices. Today, panforte remains a cherished holiday gift. You can easily divide the mixture between two springform pans—one cake to enjoy yourself and another to share with a loved one.

SERVES 8

Edible rice paper

2 1/2 cups raw almonds (350 g)

1 1/4 cups all-purpose flour (150 g)

1 teaspoon mixture of nutmeg, ground cloves, coriander, cinnamon, ginger

1 1/3 cups candied orange peel (200 g), diced

1 1/3 cups candied cedro (citron) (200 g), diced

5 dried figs, diced

2 pieces stem or crystallized ginger

1 cup confectioners' sugar (125 g), plus more to serve

3/4 cup honey (preferably miele di arancio) (180 ml)

Preheat oven to 350°F (180°C).

Line the base of a 7-inch (18-cm) springform pan with edible rice paper and the sides with parchment paper.

Roast almonds on a baking sheet at 350°F (180°C) for a few minutes.

Combine flour and spice mixture in a large bowl. Stir in roasted almonds, candied fruit, figs, and ginger until coated in flour.

Place confectioners' sugar, honey, and 3 tablespoons water in a saucepan over low heat until sugar dissolves. Bring to a boil. Then reduce heat and simmer uncovered 5 minutes.

Pour the hot syrup into fruit and nut mixture and mix quickly. Spread evenly into prepared pan, pressing lightly with the back of a spoon.

Bake at 350°F (180°C) for 30 minutes. It will be soft and appear underdone, but will firm as it cools.

Carefully remove from pan and let cool completely before slicing. Sprinkle with confectioners' sugar to serve.

Miele di arancio, orange blossom honey, is produced in Southern Italy. It is a pale yellow, delicate honey with citrus undertones.

BUCCELLATO

SICILIAN CHRISTMAS CAKE WITH FIGS AND NUTS

SERVES 12

FOR THE PASTRY

4 cups all-purpose flour, sifted (480 g)

3/4 cup sugar (150 g)

1/4 cup (1/2 stick) butter (60 g)

1/4 cup lard (50 g)

3 eggs

1 tablespoon honey

Salt

To make the pastry, pulse flour, sugar, butter, lard, eggs and a pinch of salt in a food processor until a ball of dough forms. Place on a lightly floured surface, knead gently and roll into a log shape. Cover in plastic wrap and refrigerate at least 1 hour.

I recommend letting both the pastry and the filling rest overnight in the refrigerator. The next day, you can roll out the pastry, fill and shape your buccellato, and then pop it in the oven.

In Italy, Christmas is often associated with *panettone* and *pandoro*, which are often industrially produced. Although not widely known outside of Sicily, *buccellato* is still made by hand. Its wreath shape and brightly colored candied fruit make it a stunning centerpiece for any Christmas table.

FOR THE FILLING

3 1/3 cups dried figs (500 g)

1 3/4 cups mixed candied peel (270 g)

3/4 cup almonds (100 g)

3/4 cup hazelnuts (100 g)

1/2 cup walnuts (50 g)

1/2 cup pistachios (60 g)

1 (8.5-ounce) jar fig jam (240 g)

3 tablespoons Moscato, Marsala, or Zibibbo

Zest of 1 lemon

1/4 cup solid vegetable shortening or suet (50 g)

1 teaspoon ground cinnamon

1/2 teaspoon ground cloves

3 1/2 ounces dark chocolate (100 g), grated

FOR FINISHING

1 egg, beaten

1 cup orange marmalade (300 g)

Glazed cherries, candied orange peel, and ground pistachios, to decorate

Preheat oven to 350°F (180°C).

To make the filling, chop the figs and candied peel into small pieces.

Place nuts in a food processor and pulse until finely chopped.

Stir figs, candied peel, chopped nuts, fig jam, Moscato, lemon zest, shortening, cinnamon, and ground cloves in a large saucepan over low heat about 5 minutes. Remove from heat.

When completely cool, stir in grated chocolate.

On a lightly floured surface, roll out the dough and cut into a 14x8-inch (36x8-cm) rectangle. Place filling in the center, lengthwise. Brush one long edge of the pastry with beaten egg. Carefully fold the pastry around the filling and gently roll back and forth to form a long log.

Brush beaten egg on one end and join the ends together, gently shaping the log into a wreath. Transfer to a baking sheet lined with parchment paper.

Using kitchen tweezers or pastry crimpers, pinch the dough evenly around the surface of the wreath. Brush the entire buccellato with beaten egg and bake at 350°F (180°C) for 30 to 40 minutes until golden brown.

Warm marmalade in a saucepan over low heat. Using a pastry brush, coat the entire surface of the buccellato with the warm preserves.

Decorate with glazed cherries, candied orange peel, and ground pistachios, as desired.

STRUFFOLI

Struffoli is a traditional sweet dish from Naples, consisting of marble-size pieces of deep-fried dough covered in honey. They are typically enjoyed at Christmas or Easter, but can also be found during Carnevale celebrations in February.

During Christmas, it is customary to serve struffoli in the shape of a wreath. To achieve this, place a clean glass in the center of a plate and arrange the struffoli around the glass. The honey helps the struffoli stick together, allowing the wreath to hold its shape when the glass is removed before serving.

SERVES 8 TO 10

5 cups all-purpose flour (600 g), sifted, plus more for preparation

6 tablespoons (3/4 stick) unsalted butter (85 g)

5 eggs (4 whole eggs and 1 yolk)

2 tablespoons sugar

1/4 cup limoncello (60 ml)

Zest of 1 lemon

Salt

Peanut or vegetable oil for frying

1 3/4 cups honey (420 ml)

2/3 cup candied orange peel (100 g), chopped

Rainbow sprinkles and glazed red cherries, to decorate (optional)

Mix flour, butter, 4 eggs, 1 yolk, sugar, limoncello, lemon zest, and a pinch of salt in a large bowl until a smooth dough forms. Shape into a ball, cover in plastic wrap, and refrigerate at least 30 minutes.

Form dough into 1/2-inch-diameter ropes. Cut them into 1/2-inch pieces and roll each one into a small ball. Place the marble-size pieces on a lightly floured tray, ensuring they don't touch each other.

Heat oil in a large saucepan or deep fryer.

Gently shake a small batch of struffoli in a sieve to remove excess flour, then fry in hot oil until golden brown. Remove with a slotted spoon and drain in a large bowl lined with paper towels. Repeat until all the dough has been fried.

Gently warm honey in a saucepan over low heat until it becomes thin and pourable. Remove from heat and gently stir in the fried struffoli until fully coated. Add candied orange peel and stir to combine.

Place in small individual serving bowls and decorate with rainbow sprinkles and glazed cherries, if desired.

ZABAIONE

Zabaione (also known as *zabaglione*) is a traditional Italian dessert, akin to custard but with the delightful addition of alcohol. While it is typically made with Marsala, a fortified wine from Sicily, you can also use Moscato, amaretto, Frangelico, port, rum, or brandy.

I often prepare zabaione when I have leftover yolks that I don't want to waste. It's an easy, delicious, and nutritious dessert. In Italy, zabaione has long been considered a tonic, historically given to listless children or the elderly to boost their energy. (Italian nonnas were never hesitant to give their grandchildren a bit of alcohol or coffee for medicinal purposes!)

The word *zabaione* can also generally mean a flavor. For example, you will frequently find cream fillings or gelato that have the flavor of zabaione.

Traditionally, the doses for the three ingredients are used in equal amounts, so it's a good idea to weigh your egg yolks and then adjust the amount of sugar accordingly. You can increase or decrease the amount of alcohol according to personal preference. My nonna's measurements were sometimes done using half an eggshell—for example, five egg yolks, five half eggshells of sugar, and five half eggshells of Marsala.

SERVES 4

5 egg yolks (90 g, depending on size of yolks)

1/2 cup sugar (90 g)

1/2 cup Marsala (80 to 90 g)

Biscotti, to serve (optional)

Bring a few inches of water to a simmer in a saucepan.

Place egg yolks and sugar in a stainless steel or heat-resistant bowl. Whisk until the mixture is thick and pale. Place the bowl on the slightly simmering saucepan (double boiler), ensuring the bottom of the bowl does not touch the hot water.

Add Marsala and continue to whisk until the mixture thickens, becoming light and fluffy and forming a ribbon on the surface when the whisk is lifted. It can take about 15 minutes.

Pour into 4 glasses and serve warm with biscotti, if desired.

Although it is preferred to eat zabaione immediately, it can be served warm or cold. To refrigerate, cover zabaione with plastic wrap and keep no more than two days. Whisk again quickly before serving.

CARTELLATE PUGLIESE

Though enjoyed year-round, *cartellate* are traditionally prepared during Christmastime in Puglia as they are said to represent either the halo or the linen that swaddled the baby Jesus in the manger. Similar sweets are also produced in Calabria, where they are known as *nèvole* or *crispelle*, and in Basilicata, where they are called *rosacatarre* or *crispedde*.

YIELD 2 DOZEN

Peel from 1 mandarin

1/4 cup extra-virgin olive oil (60 ml)

3 cups 00 flour (360 g)

1 teaspoon sugar

1 teaspoon baking powder

Salt

1/2 cup white wine (120 ml)

Peanut or vegetable oil for frying

2 cups honey or vincotto (480 ml)

Rainbow sprinkles, silver dragées, chopped hazelnuts or walnuts, confectioners' sugar, or cinnamon sugar, to decorate

Heat mandarin peel and olive oil in a small saucepan over low heat for a few minutes. Remove peel and let oil cool until tepid.

Mix flour, sugar, baking powder, and a pinch of salt in a bowl or on a clean surface and create a well in the center. Pour the tepid oil into the well and knead until the mixture reaches a slightly sandy texture.

Form the dough into a mound and make another well in the center. Pour in white wine and knead until you have a compact and smooth dough. Cover with a cloth or plastic wrap and let rest 30 minutes.

Working in batches, pass the dough through a pasta machine as if making pasta. Start with the notch at the widest number, reducing as you proceed. Continue until you have a very thin sheet of pastry. (Please refer to page 216.)

Using a zigzag pasta wheel, cut the dough into 10x2-inch (25x5-cm) strips. Lightly fold each strip in half lengthwise and pinch every 1 inch along the edges to create little pockets.

Wind each strip into a spiral, pinching in places to keep them intact. It's important to secure the dough well to prevent the cartellate from unfolding during frying. If the dough doesn't stick, gently moisten the parts you want to pinch together with water.

Arrange the cartellate on a tray lined with parchment paper and let sit to dry 2 hours or even overnight.

Heat oil in a saucepan or deep skillet. To check if it is hot enough, add a few pastry scraps. The oil should bubble and the pastry should float to the surface.

Fry the cartellate in batches, carefully turning once and removing when slightly golden on each side. Drain on paper towels, turning to release oil from the pockets.

Heat honey in a small saucepan over low heat. Submerge the cartellate in the honey for 1 to 2 minutes.

Remove the cartellate from the saucepan, arrange on a serving plate, and decorate as desired.

CROSTOLI

If you look in bakery windows during Carnevale in Italy, you'll see trays of thin, crispy, fried pastries dusted with confectioners' sugar. My Calabrese Nonna Concetta called them *crostoli* as they do in the northeast, but like so many Italian treats, they're known by over a dozen different names throughout the peninsula, including *chiacchiere di carnevale, cenci, frappe, sfrappe, sfrappole, bugie, stracci, fiocchi, cencetti, galani, meraviglias, teste di turchi, straccetti, nacatoli,* and *gali.* Whatever you call them, there is no denying that they are delicious and incredibly addictive. It is impossible to eat just one and you'll be surprised how quickly they disappear.

YIELD 6 DOZEN

4 cups 00 flour (480 g), sifted

1/3 cup sugar (80 g)

1 teaspoon baking powder

Salt

4 eggs (3 whole eggs and 1 yolk), lightly beaten

2 tablespoons grappa

Zest of 1 lemon

1/4 cup (1/2 stick) unsalted butter, room temperature (60 g)

Peanut or vegetable oil for frying

Confectioners' sugar, to serve

Using a stand mixer fitted with the whisk attachment, blend flour, sugar, baking powder, and a pinch of salt. Mix in lightly beaten eggs and yolk, grappa, and lemon zest until well combined. Switch to the dough hook attachment and add butter, mixing until a ball of dough forms.

On a lightly floured surface, knead dough about 10 minutes or until smooth. Add a little water if the dough seems crumbly or dry. Roll into a ball, cover with plastic wrap, and let rest 30 minutes at room temperature.

Divide the dough into quarters and work with one piece at a time. Keep the reserved dough wrapped in plastic to prevent it from drying out. Knead the dough and roll out with a rolling pin.

The next part is like making pasta. Flatten the dough with the palm of your hand and pass it through a pasta machine once on the widest setting.

Fold the dough in thirds and pass it through at the widest setting again. Repeat, adjusting the machine until the dough is very thin. (Please refer to page 216.)

Using a zigzag pasta wheel, cut the dough into 4x2-inch (10x5-cm) strips. Cut a 1-inch slit lengthwise in the center of each piece and fold one end through the slit. (Alternatively, you can leave them untwisted if you prefer.)

Let the crostoli rest while heating oil in a saucepan or deep skillet to 350°F (180°C). To check if it is hot enough, add a few pastry scraps. The oil should bubble and the pastry should float to the surface.

Working quickly, place 3 crostoli in the oil at a time. Turn and remove when they are slightly golden. Drain on paper towels. Repeat with the remaining dough.

Store in an airtight container and serve sprinkled with confectioners' sugar.

FRITTELLE DI RISO

RICE FRITTERS

Continuing with Italian Carnevale traditions, this treat is a classic, especially in Tuscany. Imagine the comforting taste of rice pudding from your childhood rolled into balls, fried to perfection, and coated in sugar. These delightful treats epitomize Italian comfort food and make a perfect accompaniment to your morning cappuccino and a cozy start to any cold winter day. If you visit "the bar" early in the day, you might be lucky enough to enjoy them fresh and hot from the deep fryer.

YIELD 3 DOZEN

1 cup pudding rice* (200 g)

1 3/4 cups whole milk (420 ml)

Zest of 1 lemon

Salt

1/2 cup sugar (100 g), plus more to serve

1/4 cup (1/2 stick) unsalted butter (60 g)

2 eggs

1 cup all-purpose flour (120 g)

Peanut or vegetable oil for frying

Ground cinnamon (optional)

* *Pudding rice is a short-grain variety that becomes soft and creamy when cooked. If you can't find it where you live, you can substitute Arborio or sticky rice.*

Place rice, milk, 1 3/4 cups water, lemon zest, and a pinch of salt in a heavy saucepan and slowly bring to a boil, stirring occasionally. Reduce heat to a simmer.

Add 1/2 cup sugar and butter and continue to simmer, stirring occasionally until rice has absorbed all the liquid.

Let cool completely, cover, and refrigerate overnight.

Remove rice mixture from refrigerator and stir in eggs, one at a time. Add 3/4 cup flour and stir until incorporated.

Using a tablespoon, scoop portions of rice and place them into a bowl of remaining 1/4 cup flour. Roll into balls and set aside.

Heat oil in a saucepan or deep fryer. Drop in a little rice mixture to check if it is hot enough (little bubbles will form around it).

Place rice balls in the oil, turning frequently to ensure even cooking. Remove when golden and drain on paper towels.

Roll in sugar (with a pinch of cinnamon, if desired) and serve warm.

For a fun twist, try mixing in 1/2 cup of sultanas (soaked in port) or some candied peel once the rice is cooked. It adds a lovely burst of flavor!

TORTA MIMOSA

SERVES 8

FOR THE SPONGE CAKE

6 large eggs

1 cup sugar (200 g)

Zest of 1 lemon

2 1/4 cups all-purpose flour (270 g)

1 1/2 teaspoons baking powder

1/2 cup (1 stick) unsalted butter (110 g), melted and cooled

FOR THE DIPLOMAT CREAM FILLING

4 egg yolks

1/3 cup sugar (65 g)

1/3 cup all-purpose flour (40 g)

1 1/2 cups whole milk (360 ml)

Zest of 1 lemon

1 cup heavy cream (240 ml)

FOR THE LIMONCELLO SYRUP

1/2 cup sugar (100 g)

1/2 cup limoncello or Cointreau (120 ml)

MAKE THE SPONGE CAKE

Preheat oven to 350°F (180°C).

Grease two 9-inch (23-cm) cake pans and line with parchment paper.

Beat eggs, sugar, and lemon zest with an electric mixer until pale, thick, and foamy.

Mix flour and baking powder and sift three times. Sift one more time directly over the egg and sugar mixture. Gently fold in the flour.

Gently stir in the butter until completely combined. Divide batter evenly between the prepared pans.

Bake at 350°F (180°C) for 25 to 30 minutes, or until a toothpick inserted into the middle of the cakes comes out clean. Turn cakes onto a wire rack to cool.

MAKE THE DIPLOMAT CREAM FILLING

Whisk egg yolks, sugar, and flour together in a bowl by hand until the mixture becomes thick and pale.

Place milk and lemon zest in a saucepan over medium heat and bring to a simmer. Remove from heat and gradually whisk a small amount of the hot milk into the egg mixture, ensuring it is fully incorporated. Repeat this step twice more. Using a spatula, transfer the egg mixture back to the saucepan with the remaining milk.

Heat over medium-low heat, continuing to whisk by hand or with an immersion blender. Gradually, the custard will thicken. Remove from heat when it starts to bubble. Transfer to a bowl and cover with plastic wrap, ensuring it sits on the surface of the custard to prevent a film from forming.

Refrigerate 2 hours or until well chilled.

Whip heavy cream until soft peaks form and gently fold into the cold custard.

In 1964, the Italian Women's Association chose the mimosa flower as the symbol for International Women's Day because it blooms in early March. On this day, mimosa flowers (acacia blossoms) are handed out to women across Italy.

Believed to have been created by a female pastry chef in Rome, *torta mimosa* is a traditional Italian dessert eaten on March 8 to celebrate International Women's Day. Its name comes from its resemblance to the mimosa flower.

MAKE THE LIMONCELLO SYRUP

Heat sugar, limoncello, and 3/4 cup water in a small saucepan over medium heat until sugar dissolves. Remove from heat and let cool. Taste and add more limoncello if desired.

ASSEMBLE THE CAKE

Using a sharp knife, trim any dark or uneven areas from the top and sides of the sponge cakes. Carefully slice each cake horizontally into three equal layers, giving you a total of six layers. Set aside three of the layers.

Place one layer of cake on a serving plate and, using a pastry brush, moisten with the limoncello syrup. Cover with 1 cup diplomat cream. Repeat layers of cake, limoncello, and cream until you have a three-layered cake. Cover with plastic wrap and refrigerate cake and remaining cream at least 2 hours.

Cut reserved layers of cake into small cubes.

Remove cake from refrigerator and cover entire top and sides of cake with diplomat cream. Place cubed cake over diplomat cream, covering the top and sides of assembled cake. Refrigerate at least 2 hours before serving.

ZEPPOLE DI SAN GIUSEPPE

In Italy, the Feast of St. Joseph on March 19 is also celebrated as Festa del Papà, or Father's Day. This day honors St. Joseph, regarded as the exemplary father figure in Christian tradition. As a result, it has become a special occasion to celebrate fathers and fatherhood throughout Italy.

YIELD 16 TO 20

FOR THE CUSTARD

4 egg yolks

1/3 cup sugar (80 g)

3 tablespoons flour (40 g)

1 3/4 cups milk (420 ml)

Zest of 1 lemon

FOR THE DOUGH

1/4 cup (1/2 stick) unsalted butter (60 g)

Salt

1 1/4 cups all-purpose flour (150 g)

4 eggs (3 whole eggs and 1 yolk)

Peanut or vegetable oil for frying

Confectioners' sugar, to serve

1 jar amarena cherries

Make the custard well in advance so it has time to cool.

To make the custard, beat egg yolks, sugar, and flour together. Heat milk and lemon zest in a saucepan and bring to a boil. Remove from heat.

Whisk 1 ladle hot milk into egg yolk mixture. Repeat until all the milk is incorporated and transfer to the saucepan over medium heat. Bring to a boil, whisking continuously as the custard thickens. Remove from heat, place in a bowl, and cover with plastic wrap, letting the plastic touch the surface of the custard to keep a film from developing. Let cool to room temperature and refrigerate.

To make the dough, place 1 cup water, butter, and a pinch of salt in a saucepan and bring to a boil.

Remove from heat and vigorously beat in all the flour at once until you have a smooth ball of dough that leaves the sides of the saucepan clean. This should take less than 1 minute.

Beat 3 whole eggs and 1 yolk together in a bowl. Measure to ensure you have 6 fluid ounces (180 ml). If you end up with a little extra, just discard it.

Using a stand mixer fitted with the paddle attachment, stir dough to lower the temperature. Slowly add the 6 fluid ounces of beaten eggs, mixing each addition in thoroughly before adding the next.

Place the pastry in a piping bag with a 12mm star tip.

Heat oil in a large saucepan or deep fryer to 350°F (180°C).

Cut several 2- to 3-inch (5- to 8-cm) squares of parchment paper and pipe a ring of pastry onto each square.

Carefully pick up the edges of the parchment paper and gently place the zeppole into the hot oil with the paper on top. After 2 to 3 minutes, use tongs to peel the paper off. Turn the zeppole a few times to ensure even cooking. Once they are golden brown, remove from the oil and drain on paper towels.

To serve, dust with confectioners' sugar, pipe custard on top, and decorate with amarena cherries.

basics

BRODO VEGETALE

VEGETABLE BROTH

Preparing broth at home ensures quality, and using genuine, natural ingredients will produce a flavorful broth far superior to any store-bought version. While purchasing broth can be convenient for a busy lifestyle (I always keep a box or two in the pantry), a little organization during the weekend can ensure you always have homemade broth on hand.

I once worked with a chef who believed that even at home, there should always be a saucepan of broth simmering on the stove. While you may not want the house smelling of broth every day, you can definitely prepare it in large quantities and freeze it in smaller portions.

Homemade broth is incredibly versatile in the kitchen. Whether you enjoy it simply in a bowl (broth is both comforting and healing) or use it as a cooking liquid to enhance the flavor of other recipes, a well-made broth warms the heart and soul.

YIELD 4 QUARTS (4 L)

1 pound carrots (455 g), coarsely chopped

1 pound onions (455 g), coarsely chopped

1 pound tomatoes (455 g), cored

5 ribs celery, leaves included, coarsely chopped

1 bunch fresh flat-leaf parsley, coarsely chopped

1 teaspoon black peppercorns

3 bay leaves

Salt

Place carrots, onions, tomatoes, celery, parsley, peppercorns, and bay leaves in a large saucepan.

Add 1 gallon cold water and bring to a boil. Reduce heat, cover, and let simmer 1 1/2 hours.

Strain and add salt to taste.

BRODO DI CARNE

MEAT BROTH

While both vegetable and meat broths are great bases for soups and risottos, a good meat broth is essential for hearty soups, risottos, stews, and sauces.

Save the pieces of meat used to make the broth. Clean the meat off the bones; it can be minced and used for pasta fillings or to add extra flavor when making tasty meatballs.

The broth will keep in the fridge 3 days and can be frozen in an airtight container for up to 3 months.

YIELD 5 QUARTS (5 L)

1 pound beef ribs (455 g)

1 pound veal shoulder (455 g)

1 pound beef or veal shank (455 g)

1 pound chicken wings, legs, and/or thighs (455 g)

5 ribs celery, leaves included, coarsely chopped

2 medium onions, coarsely chopped

2 carrots, coarsely chopped

1 leek, green part only, coarsely chopped

1 sprig fresh flat-leaf parsley

1 bay leaf

1 teaspoon black peppercorns

Coarse salt

Place beef ribs, veal shoulder, shank, chicken pieces, celery, onions, carrots, leek, parsley, bay leaf, peppercorns, and a pinch of salt in a large saucepan.

Add about 1 1/2 gallons (about 5 1/2 L) cold water and bring to a boil. Reduce heat, cover, and let simmer 3 hours.

Using a ladle or spoon, periodically skim the surface to remove impurities and fat throughout the cooking process.

Strain and once cooled, place in refrigerator. When fat has solidified on the top, remove as much as you can.

SUGO AL POMODORO

TOMATO SAUCE

When cooking Italian food, one of the most indispensable and important recipes to get right is a basic *sugo al pomodoro*—tomato sauce. The ingredients are few, but the choice of ingredients from the tomato pulp to the olive oil is important as this is often the foundation for many other recipes. And let's be honest, when you get it right, one of the best Italian dishes to eat is a simple bowl of spaghetti al pomodoro with some fresh basil and freshly grated Parmigiano Reggiano.

SERVES 4 TO 6

4 tablespoons extra-virgin olive oil

1 onion, finely chopped

1 medium carrot, finely chopped

1 rib celery, finely chopped

2 cloves garlic, peeled and smashed

2 (14-ounce) cans crushed tomatoes (400 g)

1/4 cup fresh basil

Salt and pepper

Heat olive oil in a saucepan over medium heat. Add onion, carrot, celery, and garlic. Stir until onion is soft and translucent, about 5 minutes.

Add tomatoes, basil, and salt and pepper to taste. Fill one of the empty cans with water and add to the saucepan. Bring to a boil. Then reduce heat, cover, and let simmer about 1 hour, stirring occasionally. Remove garlic cloves before serving.

This freezes well and it's so easy, you'll never buy jarred sauce again!

FOCACCIA

Italian *focaccia* is a flat-style baked bread with enough height to be sliced in half and used for sandwiches or served as a side. The dough serves as a base for various toppings like rosemary, olives, or caramelized onion. In different regions of Italy, the name and characteristics of flatbread vary—northern Italy calls it focaccia, while Rome refers to a thinner, crunchier version as *pizza bianca*.

YIELD 1 FOCACCIA

6 1/4 cups bread flour (850 g)

2 packets (1/2 ounce) active dry yeast (14 g) or brewer's yeast

1 teaspoon sugar

1 1/2 tablespoons salt

Extra-virgin olive oil

Fresh rosemary

Sea salt flakes

In the bowl of a stand mixer fitted with the dough hook attachment, mix flour with 2 1/2 cups room temperature water until fully incorporated. Cover with plastic wrap and let rest for at least 30 minutes to allow the autolyse process to begin.

In a small bowl, dissolve yeast and sugar in 1/2 cup of warm water. If using active dry yeast, let rest 5 minutes until foamy. Add to flour mixture and mix on low speed, gradually increasing to medium once most of the water is incorporated. Add salt and continue mixing for about 5 minutes.

If bowl is glass, leave dough as is. Otherwise, transfer to a lightly oiled large glass bowl. Cover with plastic wrap and let rise in a warm place for about 3 hours until more than doubled in size.

Lightly grease bottom of a 14-inch (36-cm) square baking tray with olive oil. Line with parchment paper and lightly oil the paper as well.

Transfer risen dough to the tray. Lightly oil your hands and fold the dough over onto itself twice—top to bottom, then left to right. Rub olive oil over the surface and cover with plastic wrap. Let rest 15 minutes.

Gently stretch the dough to fit evenly in the tray. Cover again with oiled plastic wrap and refrigerate overnight (or at least 8 hours).

Remove tray from refrigerator and let rest at room temperature 1 hour. The dough will rise more and bubbles should form under plastic wrap.

Preheat oven to 450°F (230°C).

Remove plastic wrap. Drizzle more olive oil over the dough and use your fingers to create dimples across the surface. Sprinkle with rosemary and sea salt flakes.

Bake on middle oven rack 20 to 25 minutes until deep golden brown.

Let focaccia rest in baking tray for a few minutes before transferring it to a wire rack. Try to resist eating all of it before it cools completely!

Store in an airtight bag overnight. To refresh, place in a hot oven 5 to 10 minutes before serving.

PASTA

Making pasta was once a daily chore, an inexpensive way to feed large families. Today, homemade pasta is usually reserved for weekends or special occasions when we have more time. Once you start making pasta, you'll quickly discover how simple and therapeutic the process is. Like the nonnas before you, with practice, you'll develop an instinct for the dough, adjusting the amount of flour or liquid as needed.

The reward of making pasta is not just in the process but the taste. You'll notice the difference. And when making pasta *ripiena* (filled pasta), you can customize the fillings. While ravioli may seem easy, it's a technique you refine over time. Once you get the hang of it, you can start experimenting with different fillings, sauces, and shapes.

In my fresh pasta recipe, I often use semola in addition to the traditional egg and "0" flour dough. Semola gives the pasta more structure, making it ideal for filled pastas or dishes like fettuccine or trofie. Semolina and semola are different: semolina is coarser, resembling cornmeal, while semola is finely ground. Semola is often used to dust fresh pasta in Italy. However, don't worry if you can't find it—you can still make excellent pasta with just flour and eggs.

The key is to knead the dough well, with plenty of effort (or *olio di gomito*, elbow grease), and then let it rest for at least 30 minutes before rolling it out. Because homemade egg pasta contains eggs, it doesn't keep long and should be refrigerated. Fortunately, it freezes well.

You can also make pasta with just flour and water, a traditional method for fresh, eggless pasta. Typically, type "0" or "00" flour is combined with water and mixed on a wooden pastry board before being rolled out with a pin. This technique yields pasta with a rough surface, perfect for capturing and holding onto sauces.

ROLLING OUT PASTA

Remove the pasta dough from the plastic wrap and cut off a piece. Rewrap the remaining dough to prevent it from drying out. Dust a clean work surface with some semolina and use your hands or a rolling pin to flatten the piece of dough.

Most pasta machines have a numbered dial that adjusts the space between the rollers to control the thickness of the dough. Usually, lower numbers indicate a thicker setting, while higher numbers make the dough thinner. (Each pasta machine is different, though—sometimes it's the opposite.) When rolling out pasta, you start with the thickest setting and progressively roll it thinner by adjusting the machine with each pass.

To begin, set the pasta machine to its widest setting. Lightly dust both sides of the dough with semola and pass it through the machine.

Next, fold both ends of the pasta sheet toward the center, creating three layers, and pass it through the machine again at the widest setting. Usually this folding is repeated three times before the pasta machine is adjusted to the next setting. Run the pasta sheet through one last time on the widest setting without folding the dough.

Now, adjust the machine to the next thinner setting. If making ravioli, I like to have the pasta sheet match the width of the machine to allow a nice width to fold over onto the filling.

Continue adjusting the machine to the next setting. The pasta sheet only needs to go through once on each setting until we reach the desired thickness. Lightly dust both sides of the sheet with semola before passing it through. For ravioli or tortellini, roll the dough until it's thin enough that you can see your hand or read newsprint through it.

PASTA ACQUA E FARINA

BASIC FLOUR AND WATER PASTA DOUGH

SERVES 2 TO 3

1 2/3 cups 00 or all-purpose flour (200 g)

Salt (optional)

On a clean surface or in a large bowl, pour the flour (and a pinch of salt, if desired) into a mound and make a well in the center.

Slowly pour ½ cup warm water (100 ml) into the well, using a fork or your fingers to gradually incorporate the flour from the edges. Continue mixing until a shaggy dough forms.

Gather the dough together and start kneading with the heel of your hand. Knead for about 8 to 10 minutes until the dough becomes smooth and elastic. If it feels too dry, add a tiny bit of water; if too sticky, dust with a little flour.

Wrap the dough in plastic wrap or cover it with a damp towel and let rest 30 minutes at room temperature. This allows the gluten to relax, making the dough easier to roll out.

Roll the dough out using a rolling pin or pasta machine to your desired thickness.

Fresh flour and water pasta cooks quickly—in about 2 to 4 minutes, depending on the shape and thickness.

PASTA ALL'UOVO

FRESH EGG PASTA DOUGH

SERVES 5 OR ENOUGH TO MAKE 4 DOZEN RAVIOLI (DEPENDING ON THEIR SIZE)

3 1/3 cups 0 or 00 flour (400 g), plus more for kneading

3/4 cup durum wheat semola (100 g), plus more for kneading

5 eggs

Salt

Sift the flour and semola together.

On a smooth surface or in a large bowl, make a mound with the blended flours and create a well in the center. Break 5 eggs into the well and add a pinch of salt.

Using a fork, gently beat the eggs, gradually drawing in flour from the inner edges of the well. Continue until the mixture thickens and becomes too difficult to mix with a fork. Use your hands to bring the dough together, incorporating any remaining flour and bits of egg.

Knead for 10 minutes, pressing and folding the dough until it becomes smooth and elastic. If the dough is too sticky, dust with a little extra flour and semola and knead lightly.

If the dough is too dry and crumbly, add a small amount of water—a teaspoon at a time—until it comes together.

Wrap in plastic wrap and let rest at room temperature for at least 30 minutes before rolling out.

For best results, refrigerate overnight if making pasta the next day.

PASTA AGLI SPINACI

SPINACH PASTA

YIELD 4 GENEROUS SERVINGS

6 ounces baby spinach (160 g)

3 cups 0 or 00 flour (400g)

1 cup durum wheat semola (140 g)

1/2 teaspoon salt

4 eggs

Sauté baby spinach in a pan over medium heat, stirring gently until all the leaves are wilted. Add 1 tablespoon water if necessary. Place in a sieve and set aside to cool completely. When the spinach is cool enough to touch, squeeze out as much liquid as you can. Purée in a food processor or blender until smooth. (You can add the eggs now or later.)

Sift the flour, semola, and salt together. On a smooth surface or in a large bowl, make a mound of the flour and create a well in the center. Pour the spinach and eggs into the well and, using a fork, incorporate into the flour until the mixture becomes too thick for the fork. Switch to using your hands, kneading the dough until it is completely smooth and slightly elastic.

The size of your eggs and the amount of liquid remaining in the spinach will affect the dough. If it appears too wet or sticky, just keep adding more flour and semola a little at a time until the pasta dough is no longer wet or sticky. Likewise, if it seems a bit too dry, add a teaspoon of water a little at a time. Knead about 10 to 15 minutes or until the pasta dough is smooth.

Cover with plastic kitchen wrap and refrigerate 30 minutes or even overnight.

The general rule when making pasta is that 100 g flour and one egg makes one portion. This is a rough estimate as eggs vary in size, but it's a good guide to use when calculating portions.

PASTA RIPIENA

FILLED PASTA

I prefer to use egg or spinach pasta when making ravioli and tortellini because the eggs create a more elastic dough that's easier to roll out and seal. The flavors also pair well with any filling you choose.

After your pasta dough has rested, roll out sheets of pasta as described on page 216. For filled pastas, the dough should be thin enough to see your hand or newsprint lines through it. I typically stop at setting number 5 on my stand mixer's pasta attachment, but please adjust as needed for your machine.

Once your first pasta sheet reaches the desired thickness, place it on a clean, well-floured surface or one dusted with semola. Since pasta dries quickly, work in batches, using one sheet at a time, and start making the filled pasta immediately. Wrap any leftover scraps in plastic wrap to knead and reuse later.

Pipe about a heaped teaspoon of filling at 2-inch intervals along one half of the pasta sheet, lengthwise. If you're using a ravioli stamp, you can lightly press it onto the sheet to create a guide for spacing the filling.

Brush water lightly around the filling to help seal the pasta. Fold the pasta sheet over the half with the filling, and gently press around each mound with your fingers to seal. Alternatively, you can use two separate sheets—one for the base and one to cover the filling. Use whichever method suits you best.

Using a ravioli stamp, glass, cookie cutter, or pasta wheel, cut out the pasta, ensuring the filling is centered in each piece. Transfer the individual pieces to a tray dusted with semola to prevent sticking.

Continue with the remaining pasta and filling. When finished, re-knead the scraps and roll them through the machine to make more.

Cook filled pasta in gently boiling water to avoid them breaking apart. They generally take 8 to 10 minutes to cook, depending on the thickness of the pasta. Test doneness by fishing out a piece with a slotted spoon and tasting it. Once ready, carefully remove the ravioli using a slotted spoon.

INDEX

Note: Page references in *italics* indicate photographs.

GRATITUDE

FIRST AND FOREMOST, my deepest gratitude to Robert Barbera for envisioning this Italian cookbook and entrusting me to bring it to life. Thank you for your trust, your passion, and for allowing me the privilege of turning this dream into reality.

To my tireless editor, Karen Richardson—where do I even begin? From our very first conversation, I knew this book was in the best hands. We were completely in sync—not only in our vision for what we wanted to create but also in our shared appreciation for the aesthetics of food photography and layout. Your patience has been nothing short of extraordinary—especially every time I insisted on redoing a food photo, left out precise measurements, or forgot to include serving sizes.

Thank you—without you, these pages might never have made it beyond my computer screen.

TONI BRANCATISANO was born and raised in Melbourne, Australia, as one of four siblings and the younger of twins. Her father, Giuseppe (Joe), was born in Calabria, Italy, to Vincenzo and Concetta, and is one of nine children (eight boys and one girl). While Vincenzo emigrated to Australia in 1950 with the two elder sons, Joe emigrated with his mother and six siblings in 1955.

After graduating as a registered nurse from the Royal Melbourne School of Nursing in 1993, Toni embarked on a working holiday in London in 1995 and her love for travel took her on an adventure that would shape her life in unexpected ways.

Originally planning to nanny two-year-old triplet girls for six months, she extended her stay in London to three years. Eventually, however, visa requirements led her to leave the country, prompting her next adventure in La Jolla, California. There, she worked for three months as a prep chef in a friend's Italian restaurant, refining her culinary skills and passion for Italian cuisine.

In August 1998, Toni arrived in Tuscany for what she thought would be her final summer abroad before returning to Australia but that plan quickly changed. A Tuscan wedding and two children later, her passion for cooking and baking flourished, and a simple hobby of creating birthday cakes for her children soon grew into a cake decorating business, making and selling cupcakes, celebration cakes, and tiered wedding cakes.

Toni's culinary talent brought her to Italy's first cooking reality show, *La Scuola—Cucina di Classe* on Gambero Rosso Channel (Sky) in 2009. After twelve weeks of intense culinary challenges, she emerged victorious, winning her own show on the network.

In 2010, she launched *Le Torte di Toni*, a cake decorating series featuring her daughter Annabella. Together, they made three series of the show, followed by two more series called *Le Torte di Toni—Masterclass*, where Toni invited guest decorators to join her each episode.

Toni's first book, *La Torta Perfetta di Toni*, was published by Gribaudo Feltrinelli Publishing in 2012.

After nearly fifteen years in Tuscany, Toni relocated to Rome, where she continued to share her love for Italian cuisine by leading group food tours and cooking classes. Her work has led to exciting roles—from guest speaking to catering for Australian and New Zealand embassy events in Rome to working as a food stylist for advertising and publicity campaigns.

Today Toni concentrates on leading bespoke, private food tours in Rome, and collaborating with travel consultants worldwide.

Toni is the proud mother of two children, Annabella and Joseph. Her journey, rooted in her love for Italian culture, food, and family, is a celebration of the unexpected paths life can take when passion and opportunity meet.

Toni's passion for cooking is a heartfelt tribute to her extraordinary mother, Roslyn. Renowned for her exquisite dinner parties, flawless table settings, and mastery of savory and sweet creations, Roslyn was the epitome of culinary elegance. Her untimely passing left an indelible mark, inspiring Toni to carry forward her legacy of love through food.

Mentoris Project
745 South Sierra Madre Drive
San Marino, CA 91108

Food styling and photography: Toni Brancatisano
Author photo: David Leigh Dodd

More information at www.mentorisproject.org

ISBN: 978-1-947431-58-4

Library of Congress Control Number: 2025934760

The recipes in this cookbook reflect traditional dishes that have been passed down through generations, adapted over time, and lovingly interpreted by the author. While every effort has been made to honor their cultural and culinary roots, these recipes are not claimed as original inventions, nor are they copied directly from any single published source.

They represent a personal approach to classic preparations, shaped by memory, experience, and taste. Any similarities to other published recipes are purely coincidental or a reflection of the shared traditions from which these dishes arise. The intent is to preserve, celebrate, and share beloved foodways—not to claim exclusive authorship over them.

This cookbook contains recipes that may include common allergens such as nuts, dairy, gluten, and shellfish. Readers are advised to be aware of their own food allergies and dietary restrictions and should consult with a medical professional if they are unsure about the suitability of any ingredients.

According to U.S. Department of Agriculture guidelines, it is important to cook food to the proper internal temperatures to ensure safety. Poultry should be cooked to an internal temperature of 165°F (74°C), while ground meats like beef, pork, veal, and lamb should reach 160°F (71°C). Steaks, roasts, and chops of beef, pork, veal, and lamb should be cooked to 145°F (63°C) and allowed to rest for at least 3 minutes before serving. Fish and shellfish should also reach 145°F (63°C), and egg dishes should be cooked to 160°F (71°C). Leftovers and casseroles should be reheated to 165°F (74°C). Always use a food thermometer to check for doneness.

The cooking methods and techniques described in this book should be followed with care. Always handle kitchen equipment and ingredients safely. The author and publisher are not responsible for any injuries, illnesses, or accidents that may occur as a result of following these recipes.

Handpainted artichoke (page 174) and fish (page 189) plates by Matilde Argiolas Porcelain Art.

Publisher's Cataloging-in-Publication
(Provided by Cassidy Cataloguing Services, Inc.)
Names: Brancatisano, Toni, author, photographer.
Title: An Italian kitchen : a celebration of seasonal and traditional Italian cuisine / Toni Brancatisano.
Description: San Marino, CA : The Mentoris Project, [2025] | Includes index.
Identifiers: LCCN: 2025934760 | ISBN: 9781947431584 (hardcover)
Subjects: LCSH: Cooking, Italian. | Seasonal cooking--Italy. | LCGFT: Cookbooks. | BISAC: COOKING / Regional & Cultural / Italian. | COOKING / Seasonal. | COOKING / Farm to Table.
Classification: LCC: TX723 .B73 2025 | DDC: 641.5945--dc23

Printed in the U.S.A.